The Match
And The Spark

Library of Congress Control Number: 2023931342

ISBN (paperback): 978-1-956450-47-7
ISBN (eBook): 978-1-956450-48-4

 Armin Lear Press Inc
215 W Riverside Drive, #4362
Estes Park, CO 80517

The Match
And The Spark

A TRANSPLANT VICTORY

Casey Bradley Gent

To **Beau** *who keeps me humble and eternally answers with I love you, too. Your hugs give me life. Thank you for allowing me this expression of what you have overcome.*

To **Bailey** *my cheerleader and Microsoft expert. May we always own big girl shoes and wear them, in celebration of womanhood, together.*

To **Beck** *for understanding big feelings. Hands down owner of the very best giggle.*

Acknowledgments

This book was written on paper, by hand, through pen and pencil. Old school style. Sometimes thoughts and memories bombarded me when the only thing nearby to write on was the back of a greeting card or a fast-food napkin.

To my husband, Greg, you are everything to each of us. Thank you for your patience with my writing. Thank you for allowing me to share the tiniest piece of your humble heroic essence. I know you would be most content as an anonymous hero. Through the process of this book, you found me cross legged on the bed, scribbling in the bath, and scratching notes on the back of Beck's artwork. Still, you never quit supporting my final goal of writing a book that would connect families with sick kids to the ideas of hope, miracles and to no wasted days. I will follow you, step at a time, to eternity.

To Sarah and Wynde. Thank you for always showing up.

To my agent, Syd. You believed in this manuscript after only reading three rough chapters. Thank you for helping me find the way. I am grateful for your vision. I am grateful for you never giving up.

To my editor, Maryann. You have never lost sight of the spark. Having a woman as my editor is a dream realized for the little girl version of my fifty-year-old self. You are proof that female writers are successful writers. Thank you for the freedom to fight for the heart of this book, which is family. Thank you for making me better.

To my parents, Debbie and Mark. Thank you for making it important and cool to be a writer!

To Kris. Your understanding of a parent's journey through their child's medical crisis is transcendent. One million thank yous.

To Shayla Marin for a great headshot.

To Alexandra Munteanu for completing the organ donation graphic.

Finally, to getting outdoors in the Colorado wild. There is nothing more healing to my tired mind and spirit.

Preface

I'd been looking at my son Beau's back for four city blocks. Walking as briskly as possible in two-inch heels, I'm trying to keep up without looking like I was trying too hard to keep up. We were in Washington, DC Proudly overlooking the National Mall, the Capitol – with strong pillars holding the white stone walls upright and grand rows of windows that looked out over the world likewise eyes –– cast a shadow across everything in its path. Beau and I walked in the shadow, along the iconic waterway, and I took in the smells of the city.

The air hinted at the smell of a ballpark, salty but bitter, and car exhaust mingled with the scent of people on the move. Beau was on a mission to visit the Holocaust Museum.

The stories and the history that awaited us there beckoned him with urgency.

"Let's stop and grab and quick drink!" I called. It was sunny and still warm for September. Even further ahead, I noticed an ice cream truck parked at the base of the Washington Monument. Tourists moved around the landscape like little armies. Beau wouldn't stop for a drink. Mostly, when his mind was set on something, Beau wouldn't stop.

"You know what you always say," he called over his shoulder, half-smiling, "you can rest when you're dead."

He was right. I did like to say that. I'd been *roasted*. Called out! There would be no drink break.

Four months before our trip to Washington, DC, Beau and I had looked out the window of his room in Children's Hospital in Aurora, Colorado and renewed our commitment that every day we lived on the other side of that glass would be a day not wasted. He was hospitalized with failing kidneys, but I'd held up a paper cup of Pepsi and Beau had tipped the edge of his water cup in my direction.

"To days that are worth waking up for!" We toasted. "To no wasted days!"

Six months before chasing my oldest son through the historic passages of DC, I was sleeping next to him on a plastic couch; shocked and mentally numb. We were patients at Children's Hospital. At 19, Beau was considered a child in the eyes of the medical world, and his routine blood work was flagged by the kidney team, professionally known as nephrologists, who found Beau was in acute kidney failure. The most significant blood marker identifying kidney trouble is creatinine. Average healthy adults have a creatinine level of .05 to .09. Beau's was 3.1, and on the outside, his normally slender athletic legs were each the size of Aspen tree trunks. His feet were fat and puffy, and because his kidneys weren't filtering the toxins from Beau's blood, he threw up nearly every hour. This part of acute kidney failure, the doctors explained, wasn't necessarily typical.

Our family had a lot to learn about typical. Failing kidneys hadn't just meant that Beau stopped making pee. In fact, the physical symptoms of acute kidney failure didn't look like I'd imagined. Beau didn't have chalky skin or a yellow tinge to the whites of his eyes. I'd only known one other person, a child whose family was clients at my portrait studio, with failing kidneys. Beau's sick didn't look like their daughter's sick. I wondered, did acute kidney failure look like any single thing, or did it look like everything? The flu, high blood pressure, swelling, cramping, puking; strange symptoms came and went.

Inside the sunny hospital room, Beau maintained his diligent study habits. Child patients are allowed to wear normal clothes. Beau had on shorts and a Patagonia T-shirt. If I didn't glance at his puffy red ankles and huge swollen toes, I might have assumed he was symptom-free. In the haze of being admitted to Children's, the hospital policy advocating street-clothes for my sick child felt empowering. We were in a health crisis. Beau's world was out of his control.

The days were out of his control, yet somehow – just being able to keep on the clothes he owned—lent a gift of stability. Hospital gowns can feel like a fabric reminder of sickness and the last thing Beau wanted was to feel enveloped in disease. Normal clothes were a symbol of normalcy. Keeping up with college homework was normal. Everything else, surreal.

Thankfully, during our four-day stint at Children's Hospital, one of Beau's most dangerous symptoms was brought under control. For a couple of days prior to being hospitalized, Beau woke up to the sour taste of bile and an urgent need to vomit. His nausea lasted most of each day. Within the walls of Children's, his team of doctors first tried a drug called Phenergan. No help. Magic Mouthwash was another anti-nausea mix Beau choked down. It was a liquid concoction of Benadryl, Maalox, and lidocaine.

Nothing. The benefit of being treated at Children's was their team approach. Four nephrologists consulted on Beau's treatment, and in their attempt to find a successful anti-nausea medication, one of the quieter Docs suggested Beau try an oral medication called Marinol, which contains a compound found in marijuana.

"Are any of you opposed to this?" Doctor Drew asked, eying Beau, his sister, Bailey, and each of us who circled the room.

"If it means Beau's able to keep a graham cracker down, we aren't opposed to trying anything!" I replied, on behalf of the family.

The drug contains a synthetic form of tetrahydrocannabinol (THC), the main psychoactive constituent of marijuana. The tiny red, FDA-approved pills were formed into perfect little beads. They rolled around in the palm of my hand when I prepared them with a cup of water for Beau. His constant trips to the toilet were taking a toll. Beau was on board with the somewhat experimental drug, and it worked like magic. With this small victory, we held onto hope. Following the first dose of Marinol, Beau slept seven peaceful hours.

Acute meant temporary. *Acute* meant treatable. *Acute* was simply a medical sabbatical,

along the road back to normalcy. *Acute*, we thought, was the golden ticket of Beau's diagnosis.

Instinctively, I had begun searching the Internet for information on kidney disease, and my reading emphasized the notion that we were suddenly now part of an alarmingly large community. Kidney disease doesn't distinguish: It affects both children and adults. While I didn't envision us staying members of the kidney community for long, I read one in seven people is impacted by kidney disease. "How could this be?" I wondered. A website I searched called *kidney.org* estimated 37 million Americans endure chronic kidney disease. I'd been clueless. And, overnight, became the parent of yet another kidney patient.

My own heart and stomach had grown knotted with

empathy for every time I watched my child's swollen bare feet balance heavily beside the toilet bowl as he puked. Marinol significantly interrupted Beau's pattern of vomiting. It provided the best kind of relief; the type of hope where Beau could focus on studying, reading and even eating. He was immediately placed on a kidney friendly diet, which removed potatoes, bananas, and sodium from his menu. In the short term, he went one entire sleep and a long morning before throwing up. I celebrated him holding down a packet of low sodium crackers and a box of apple juice. The second milestone Beau hit was 24 hours without an episode of hanging his head dutifully over the toilet.

I admired Beau. I longed to pick him up and cradle his 145-pound failing body. He endured, and the progress brought by Marinol felt fantastic! Finally, late in the morning on a Monday, we checked out of our room on the sixth floor of Children's Hospital. The state of Beau's kidney health was undetermined. He basked in the simple short-term victory of no more nausea.

We had two vehicles waiting in the parking lot. Beau would drive his little gray Mazda van twenty minutes back to college at Regis University, and I would not ride shotgun. This left a heavy lump in my throat, and for a moment I doubted both my strength and Beau's resiliency. Letting my sick child resume his life back at college seemed crazy – off the charts reckless.

"Be brave," I repeated to myself. We were on the outside of the glass now. "God," I prayed, "Please take away some of this worry, help me carry it, and give Beau the strength of the mountains."

There wasn't really a middle ground when it came to Beau leading a normal life. I couldn't move into the dorm, and Beau wouldn't put the brakes on his life as a 19-year-old college student. In the midst of his diagnosis, we remained determined to not abandon our dreams. We embraced the gift of normal days. At the red traffic light outside of Children's, Beau and I sat inside our separate vehicles, waiting. He looked eager for the light to change quickly. I was content, watching him through the glass.

Predictably, the red light didn't last forever. Once the color changed, Beau and his tiny van headed North at the Interstate. I turned South, toward home. He tooted a goodbye. I cried. I searched the Internet for articles and remedies, for any tidbit about kidney failure with a bright ending. I felt like Beau's sudden onset of this terrible sickness was my fault, or that maybe, if I had fed him more cranberries and fewer chicken nuggets as a little guy, I could have prevented this. I felt guilty for my child's diagnosis.

During one Google marathon, I came across the kidney advocacy group called Nephcure, which was was looking for essay entries into a contest about life in the Kidney Community. Contest winners would receive an all-expenses paid trip to Washington, DC.

"Well," I thought, fingers crossed, "We won't be part of this group for long. We won't need to be, once Beau's kidneys recover, but I can write about this moment and feeling wrecked."

Just before going to bed, I mentioned the contest to my husband, Greg.

"You should enter!" He encouraged. "Seriously, Casey, do it!"

Greg stood against our bathroom vanity, shaving like a wild man, with Colgate cream bouncing off the sink and into the mirrors. God, I loved him.

"You're cute." I replied, studying my husband of nearly twenty-five years. He was tanned and fit. Wrinkles formed in the soft skin around the corners of his turquoise eyes.

"Do it." Greg smiled, easily. "Write an essay. You think about Beau's diagnosis *all* the time."

He flicked a speck of shaving cream off the razor in my direction. We both laughed as I wiped it away. For the rest of the night, I stayed awake – writing. Words flew off my Sharpie onto the paper and, once again, I cried. My writing was an unraveling. I had no idea where we'd go from here. I poured everything about Beau's struggle into a notebook and was forced to admit that I was scared for my child every single day.

The following week, my essay was chosen as one of Nephcure's winners. Beau and I were going to DC! Winning the essay contest didn't turn out to be the end of the line with my writing. Our trip to DC introduced Beau and me to ten other contest winners who were also enduring kidney failure. These people came alive; they became more than faceless members of a community that I couldn't wait to leave. One girl was a dancer. Another member of this kidney community had received a lifesaving transplant just three weeks earlier. She was thirteen; I continued writing for this hero and for myself. I wrote for everyone who faces a grave illness, and simply needs to read that one diagnosis does not define a human being's spirit.

This is Beau's story. Living through it changed me forever. Beau doesn't linger in the past or talk about it very much either. He lives for today. He lives for *this* day, studying to work in the medical field, playing Spike ball in the summer grass, and internally wondering why his Momma spends so much time focused on what was. Beau has little time for looking back.

My 22-year-old child carries the purple stretch marks from forty pounds of water weight that he put on in the first six weeks of kidney failure. He wears the port scar in his chest where blood was ferried in and out of a dialysis machine. Beau owns the pain, medical battles, and victories. I didn't write this book to move

Beau backward, for in every step of our family's journey, he chose forward.

I wrote this book for all the times I was weak because in weakness, I discovered the absolute core of empathy. I gained knowledge in the form of asking other patients "How are you *this morning*?" As opposed to asking, "How's is the battle?" Medical battles are won in moments. Progress is achieved by little victories.

I also wrote this book to share what I learned through enduring my son's pain. I learned **endurance** is both beautiful and hard, that it exists in waves, and it is fluid. I don't think anybody who loves someone sick can ever go cold-turkey on endurance. Endurance sat right there, as Beau struggled, for me to lean on. In the moments when I could not change Beau's diagnosis, my personal cadence became the words: Wrecked is not broken.

For anyone caring for a loved one with a serious medical diagnosis, I hope my candor in the following pages gives you a Free Pass to feel scared, mad, hopeful too, and even wrecked. I don't want any reader to lie in bed alone and try to sleep away their grief. Hold onto faith, hold onto the helpers who show up every day like you do, and hold onto small medical victories.

There were pinnacle moments, for me, while Beau's kidneys were failing. One was in January, on the Star Wars adventure ride at Disneyland. Our entire family bobbed in and out between sand dunes – we bounced around in a spacecraft fleeing some bad guy. We were jedis. Beau existed as one big smile. His hair was on fire. The five of us had three minutes to lose the world and we did. That one silly ride was a monumental victory for the kid on dialysis. It was a momentary victory over sickness for our whole grieving family. But as you'll discover, there were infinite times during Beau's grave illness when the Momma in me wished I could carry his disease and found I might not have the faith or stamina to do it.

— 1 —
Not a Pretty Picture

In the pictures on my cell phone, there's a photo of a little boy I don't know. He is unsteady – thin as a rail, as my Grandma Bradley would have said – and balancing on a physical therapist's trapeze. The trapeze is nothing more than a simple gray step, maybe six inches off the ground, but to this little boy it may as well be a circus highwire. His eyes look sunken and hollow, but he stands. He is smaller than other boys his age and his shoulder blades sink forward from the weight of standing. A baggy, black T-shirt conceals physical frailty, yet this boy stands. He balances. He is not broken.

The photo on my cell phone is of my son Beau at thirteen. When I snapped the blurry image of this difficult era in our lives, I had no idea that Beau and I would visit it often; that it would become a touchstone for each of us of this life that is precarious, barely hanging on, and nearly tipping over, but not broken.

I felt like an outsider when I snapped the picture: ashamed as a professional photographer, because the photo wasn't good to look at, and failed as a momma, because none of it was pretty. It showed everything hard. For the second time in his life, Beau was experiencing a medical crisis, and exposing raw emotion is just what any grave medical diagnosis does. It plunges us straight into a situation that is not immediately fixable. A grave diagnosis sets us into the hard, and we cannot simply photoshop the moment away. We must sit there, in despair and discomfort. We must also, when we are able, allow our loved one's diagnosis to become one image of him and not the only image.

Beau was a newbie to the physical therapy prescribed for boosting his fragile muscles, and the ugly snapshot on my cell phone was different from every other portrait I had captured of him. Usually, Beau was smiling, or being silly. His eyes were always bright and his demeanor, confident. This was the first image in which Beau was fighting with all of his mind and faith to be considered anything but *sick*. His eyes didn't connect in this photo. Beau's face was turned down in defeat, but the picture was important. He was struggling, off balance on the physical therapist's wooden beam and out of focus, but not flattened.

Until he turned nine, Beau's hair was an unreal shade of blonde. It was white gold, the likes of no other head of hair I've ever seen, and on family vacations to San Francisco and Honolulu, Hawaii, Japanese tourists surrounded Beau two different times to photograph him. Several times, strangers stopped and rubbed their fingers through his bright shock of hair. Travelers explained to us, more than once, that a boy with hair the shade of Beau's was lucky – even Godlike. Once, when he was four, Beau held his hand up to a family of tourists who were snapping shots of him at the beach.

"Stop!" his scratchy little voice requested. "Please. No more picachures."

It never once struck me as creepy that people from other cultures were enamored with Beau. We all were! As a little boy, he was very blonde, very tan, and very smiley. Beau was also very sweaty. He hadn't turned two years old when his daddy, my husband Greg, pulled the car over to toss an incredibly stinky pair of Beau's socks out the driver's side window into a roadside trash can. We all giggled hysterically and plugged our noses. Beau's older sister, Bailey, danced around in her car seat next to him, asking how in the world someone *so small* could stink *so big*? Our first son was constantly busy, had a smile that melted us, a stunning face, and an unwaveringly steady disposition. He was forever unruffled – a golden boy with golden hair until he hit thirteen and his health began to change. While his demeanor remained unshakable, everything else about Beau was different. Even his blonde hair darkened, with just a streak of gold remaining at his temple.

Beau had complained of a backache for several days. His back ached so badly, in fact, that he missed almost a week of baseball practice, opting instead to lie stiffly on the couch. All of him seemed to be stiff. In the early mornings, I had watched him walk gingerly from the carpool into school while other seventh grade boys jogged past him. That was unusual. Beau liked to move with purpose, and he didn't like to be last.

"Puberty?" Greg and I lamented Beau's unlikely symptoms. We lay in bed one night, and I wondered out loud if our normally vivacious Colorado kid just had a nasty case of the flu. Though I tried not to be consumed by worry, I couldn't shake it. There is a kind of worry, when it comes to my children, that undermines my brain and shakes the very center of my momness.

Beau's physical exam the following Tuesday revealed only that he was underweight. He shared with the doctor that his arms and legs and back almost always ached. Our doctor suggested that running some bloodwork might ease our concerns. We left the office after a nurse drew several vials of blood from Beau's left arm. It was his first experience having blood drawn.

For the next few nights, I began a routine of massaging Beau's back after dinner time to ease his stiffness. Thankfully, he had not become too cool for many of the things that always connected us. My boy loved a shoulder rub. When he was a toddler, Beau loved for me to gently rub my nails along his sides just underneath his jammies. He almost never, at any age, refused a back rub.

On this Friday night, I started to gently knead Beau's neck. Sometimes, Greg would tease us – sticking his feet into the mix. Greg's toes were long, with a few stray hairs that popped up here and there. It always made Beau laugh.

"I need a massage, too!" Greg would cackle. However, on this night in the overstuffed chair next to us, he and our two-year-old son, Beck, were engrossed in a seek-and-find book about Disney's Nemo. We were all cozy underneath colorful fleece blankets. The living room felt warm and smelled like the hazelnut syrup from Greg's coffee. The grip of worry started to release me.

Then my fingers found the lump, and more lumps. My heart thumped hard and fast. Quickly, I double checked my steps. It didn't matter which side of Beck's neck I traced my way down; from the base of Beau's dusty blonde hairline to either side of his spine – left side, right side – it didn't make a difference. Beneath my Momma-fingers, Beau's fragile shoulders were covered with rock-hard lymph nodes. Eight hardened lymph nodes the size and shape of almonds lay everywhere underneath my boy's skin. "The ER," I mouthed to Greg. "We have got to get Beau to the hospital."

This was the earliest episode in Beau's medical mystery when having our daughter Bailey, then a sophomore in high school, saved little Beck. Bailey was not typical in the sense of teenagers who ache to be away from home. Instead, she always jumped at the chance to cuddle Beck or laugh with him over the crazy selfies those two would capture in their moments together. Loving Beck gave Bailey great purpose.

Bailey is thirteen years older than her littlest brother and just two and half years older than Beau. As elementary school kids, Bailey and Beau nitpicked constantly. Even ten-minute car rides were a battle over listening to Taylor Swift instead of The Foo Fighters. When Bailey refused to apologize for something she had done, Beau would plead with his stubborn sister to simply say "I am sorry" rather than being punished and sent to her room for being disrespectful. Generally, Beau's kind-hearted pleas didn't work.

Before middle school, Bailey was the queen of stand-offs, leaving either Greg or me left standing mid-sentence behind a slammed door. She was a pro at being sent to her room. For a particularly snarky stretch of two weeks, we removed the door to Bailey's bedroom from its hinges to prevent the incessant slamming. In the gap between Bailey's birth and Beck's delightful arrival, our stubborn daughter found her one true love. With a baby in the house, Bailey's focus turned from herself to him. On the night I discovered Beau's lumps, Bailey was genuinely glad to cuddle and babysit her littlest brother. "My favorite human" she called him. Bailey asked me to call her with an update from the hospital as soon as possible.

As we shuffled our way into the car, Beau hung his chin on his chest. I still picture his feet shuffling along the hardwood floor. He was too weak to lift his legs. Beau began to complain that it was hard to breathe. This was new. We propped him up on pillows and a hand-sewn quilt in the back seat. Greg gingerly began the twenty-five-minute drive to the nearest ER. If there is such a thing as gingerly and wild abandonment combined, then that is how Greg got us to the hospital.

When we reached the hospital, the attending physician was measurably concerned about Beau's presentation. Presentation was a medical term for how the *patient* looked and acted. As the Momma, I was just as concerned with the doctor's presentation as I was with Beau's. It was either: *Yes*, this doctor understood our urgency, or *Nope*, this doctor didn't get it, and we'd need to find another physician ASAP. Fortunately, the doctor who greeted us "got it."

Beau's oxygen levels were fine, but the lethargy combined with the lumps was not.

Beau was rushed from a small admittance room for a CT scan. We were not allowed to accompany him. This was the first and last time Greg or I would ever leave Beau in the care of doctors without one of us present. We made a parent pact, because the twenty-five-minute CT scan left Beau with no advocate.

> **Every hospital patient needs an advocate, especially a child.**

Following Beau's CT scan, the doctor explained: "Exactly **not** what we expected to find. Which is really good." He clutched his hands in his lap and let go of a long, relieved sigh. "Your boy's body is not riddled with cancer."

The numerous swollen lymph nodes in Beau's neck had worried all of us. *Riddled with cancer.* Initially, the words felt like big heavy logs to me, but then the word *cancer* took on a nonsensical taste: bitter, salty on the sides of my tongue; hard to swallow. The word *cancer* even had a temperature – hot. Greg, Beau, and

I sat smashed inside a tiny patient room in the Children's ER. On one wall, an enormous purple painting of Eeyore showed Eeyore trying to smile. The corners of Eeyore's mouth curled just barely, but they failed. Eeyore always failed. Sitting there, I felt like Eeyore. I sat up, tried to listen like a big girl, and couldn't quite get it done. *Riddled with cancer.* The words stuck in my brain. I tapped my feet rapidly and looked at the ground as the doctor continued talking.

Even though Beau's CT scan was promising, and the doctor did *not* see cancer, I couldn't get rid of the dread that sat in the bottom of my belly. Beau's symptoms had appeared so randomly and with so much aggression! The doctor said that after feeling Beau's neck, and performing the initial exam, he had fully expected to see lit-up lymph nodes spread throughout our son's body. When I asked him to explain more, I learned that in cancer patients who undergo MRI or CT scans, there is often a glowing line around tumors or growths. The glowing lines represent cancer cells that are changing and morphing. Beau's CT scan showed none of that. There were neither glowing lines nor the presence or existence of tumors. This seemed like a victory, but victory over what? The culprit had no name.

We didn't have a diagnosis, nothing concrete to label Beau's symptoms, and I worried about everything that was left unanswered. Why did he have so many enlarged lymph nodes? When he shuffled into the ER, why could Beau barely breathe? While one scary disease had been eliminated from the list, we were left with an enemy the doctor couldn't identify, and I wondered, which was worse? Was it harder to fight cancer, or to fight a battle with an invisible adversary? I wanted nothing more than to be grateful, but I was worried. Greg wrapped his arm around me and pulled my body tight against his side. "Relax. This is good." He said. "Beau's gonna be just fine."

We left the ER with very few answers. We also left the ER with a drug that helped Beau

a lot: prednisone, a steroid. This hospital visit was, for lack of a better term, our first rodeo. And for Beau, receiving an intravenous dose of prednisone (following his CT scan) became a jumpstart back to health, although negative effects of the drug can include extreme anxiety, anger, the inability to control anger, acne, poor sleep, immunosuppression, and even water weight that's carried in the face and across the forehead. In fact, a lot of moms of prednisone kids will yell at this page as they read it. Believe me, I understand the yelling. "Prednisone is a crutch!" The detractors say. "Doctors throw prednisone at dangerous symptoms when they're guessing."

Hold tight, Mommas, one immense *benefit* of the steroid can be the speed with which it works.

Beau's improvements following his first infusion were instant. The pain in his lungs subsided. His joints weren't achy, or at least the ache did not overpower him. Best of all, Beau left the ER walking fully upright – no chin on chest, no stiffly bending knees. When we were discharged from our visit, and the doctor handed me a paper script for more prednisone, I literally carried the paper like a fresh one-hundred-dollar bill. I neither folded it nor tucked it away. Had I been handed a script for acetaminophen, that may not have even made it to the trash pile in the bottom of my purse. But this was prednisone. It worked like a magical potion, and we had a script to get more! I carried it like a delicate flower.

— 2 —
Code Breakers and Doctor Visits

Even though Beau had been declared cancer-free, we soon began seeing a cancer specialist at Children's Hospital Colorado. Beau's bloodwork from several weeks earlier showed numerous red flags. The medical world uses the term "markers," and Beau's markers indicated that medical follow-up was required. However, the markers did not spell out exactly what specialty could help him. I wished that all the codes in all our bodies spoke English, or Arabic, or Spanish, or some other kind of universal language that all the best experts in medicine could decipher – harmoniously. Instead, our bodies speak with a code that can be elusive, subjective, left up to debate and even uncrackable.

One real conundrum in the modern riddle of getting to a solid medical diagnosis is autoimmune diseases. When I think about a familiar autoimmune disease, I think about something as common as my great grandmother's rheumatoid arthritis. It would not be unfair for me to state that in the last two years, there have at least fifty occasions when I have listened to a friend or acquaintance (diagnosed with an autoimmune disease) explain how it took multiple doctors years to decipher their body's code and unravel their disease. Every single day, someone new embarks upon the deciphering stage of their medical diagnosis. Patients, parents of patients, and physicians: We are the decoders. Beau did not have cancer, yet in what seemed to be a random process, he became a patient in the cancer and blood disorders clinic. It wasn't that Beau was placed there without great thought or good intention. Beau was placed in the wrong specialty because of a shortage in code breakers.

The biggest revelation at our first Cancer Center appointment was Beau's blood platelet count of five. "It is okay.," Doctor Shirley assured us. "Once I had a patient with a platelet count of two." Dr. Shirley was excellent at talking directly to Beau. I listened over Beau's shoulder but had nothing to give me perspective. If ten was a normal platelet count, I figured that five wasn't too far off. Perspective, as the parent of a sick kid, is elusive. I feel really great about myself as a mother on the days when I can translate medical terminology. Alternatively, I try not to berate myself on the all-too-common days when I'm forced to ask Google for a detailed explanation of Beau's next treatment.

"What is a normal platelet count?" Beau asked.

Following the ER visit, he was very tuned in to his own care, and he was feeling better with continued doses of prednisone.

"Well," Dr. Shirley paused, "140,000 plus platelets per microliter is considered normal."

She watched him intently for a reaction. So did I. And Beau brought us his great big toothy smile.

"I guess I can't get much worse." He said.

They both giggled. Then Dr. Shirley became more serious.

"As long as your count is below 10, you won't be able to play football or wrestle. Nothing too physical." She patted Beau's shoulder and finished by saying, "I think the numbers will start to go up. Come see me again next week for another blood draw. "In my mind, these numbers did not make sense.

Beau stood up to walk out of the exam room and apparently, I just sat there, glazed over. Zero perspective.

"Mom?" Beau whispered, "Time to go."

"Dr. Shirley," I asked, "what exactly do Beau's platelets do? What is their purpose?"

The responsibility of being the POP (parent of a patient), as opposed to *being* the patient, is twofold. I am both advocate and decoder. More and more often I found myself addressing doctors with specifics about Beau as if my son were the only human patient in their practice. I did not ask what purpose platelets served in general, but what purpose they served for my son. Parents with sick kids develop a very singular focus: how do we keep all the parts of this child's miracle body working?

"Platelets are responsible for blood clotting." Dr. Shirley explained. "I don't want to see Beau take a big fall or play contact sports. I would be worried about stopping him from bleeding." I started thinking, "I don't want to see Beau leave my direct line vision." I began to cry. The tears gathered outside of my eyelids, and I could not stop their fall.

A tear that is shed may be clear, but it is not invisible, and I could not hide my sad heart from Beau. I know he saw that I was crying, but he continued the discussion with purpose.

"How about baseball?" Beau asked.

"You should definitely go to practice and play catch with your dad." Dr. Shirley replied.

She knew that baseball was the bond Beau shared with Greg. The one time she met Greg, Beau introduced him by saying, "Here is my dad. He is a great baseball coach."

Dr. Shirley also recognized something that I was still learning in this journey: sick kids cannot live their lives on hold. People who are sick are just like people who are well. We must all have things to look forward to, and projects to undertake, and for someone fighting a grave diagnosis, the normal aspects of life must get woven into the patient's treatment plan just like another blood draw, infusion, or check-up.

When I was little, my Daddy liked to say everybody needs a reason to get up in the morning. Everybody doesn't mean just the folks in perfect health. I embraced the quote more fully as a mother. Everybody means every single body – the sick, the well, and the healing. Every day is a fresh start with a chance to do something new, or in Beau's case, a chance to do just what he loved best, that is, play ball. Even as a pre-teen, Beau refused the chance to waste time or waste an opportunity. I frequently told him and Bailey they could rest when they were dead. Mostly, I wanted them to live big and dream bigger. Beau wanted no wasted days.

We left the office carrying the weight of a platelet count 135,000 points below normal. Realistically, I was the one who carried the weight of the worry. As we walked to our car, Beau grinned and simply said, "See, I can still go to baseball."

— 3 —
Autoimmune Disease and Flare-ups

We weren't more than two months into Beau's care when Dr. Shirley told us she was moving to Asheville, North Carolina.

"And you can't follow me there." She smiled. "Plus, I am not really getting you the answers you deserve."

Dr. Shirley was an up-and-comer. She looked to be just a couple of years out of medical school, with a soothing demeanor, grace with my teenager, and the figure of Dr. Meredith Gray from television's *Grey's Anatomy*. On more than one of our visits, Dr. Shirley's expertise was requested for a patient in a neighboring hospital room. Her colleagues liked and respected her. It turned out that young Dr. Shirley was leaving to lead the Children's Cancer unit in Asheville. Even with all that was going on in her life, she had found time to do some homework regarding Beau's low platelet count and unusual symptoms.

"I want you to see a colleague of mine named Dr. Marsh." Dr. Shirley explained. "You don't have all the markers of a disease called Lupus, but you have at least three of them. And," she emphasized, "Dr. Marsh knows a whole ton about Lupus."

At this point, the only thing I knew about Lupus was that

one of my photography clients had it. She had to cancel and reschedule a photo shoot once because of a "flare-up." We learned that Dr. Marsh would see Beau in one week, and with a tight hug, Dr. Shirley ushered us into a new phase of care for Beau. With no medical intervention besides daily doses of prednisone, Beau was having more good days. The weekly blood draws, where even seasoned phlebotomists struggled to successfully stick Beau's disappearing veins, were revealing a skyrocketing platelet count. Good. Great, really. The most disheartening symptom these days was that Beau continued to vomit daily.

Following our goodbye with Dr. Shirley, Beau and I stopped at a bookstore. I wanted to find a book about Lupus. After we arrived home and I had settled in with my new book, the explanation of Lupus wasn't any clearer. It seemed like, if I found a hundred people with Lupus and asked about their symptoms, I might get a hundred different answers. Lupus looked different on everyone. I retained two facts: Lupus was an autoimmune disease and it mostly affected women. Additionally, getting to a Lupus diagnosis could be a long and winding journey.

Once we set eyes on Dr. Marsh, it was immediately evident to me that she was a medical rock star. Dr. Marsh was four feet ten inches of encyclopedic medical knowledge and the number one reason that Dr. Marsh was a rock star: she was not an alarmist. She explained that she wouldn't be big on setting limits for Beau.

"Wait, no curfews?" I teased. Her job would be the opposite of curfews, it would be the opening of windows and the unlocking of doors. Dr. Marsh wanted to enable Beau with the health to be a normal teenager. I think Beau and I both loved that! We exchanged looks and I settled back into my chair with eager ears.

During our first appointment, Dr. Marsh asked Beau to bend at the waist, reach down, and touch his ankles. Beau did as he was instructed but could barely reach down to touch his knees. He glanced up at us both, embarrassed. Several additional interactions showed that Beau had the flexibility of a wooden clothespin, that is, none.

"Not to worry." Dr. Marsh encouraged. "A lot of teenage boys are not very flexible."

She also went on to explain that if Beau did have Lupus, his body would mistake its own tissue as invasive. In that case, he would have inflamed tissue that created stiff joints and poor flexibility.

"Hmmm." Beau reflected. "I've definitely had many days with stiff joints. Mostly my knees."

"And the good news, "Dr. Marsh replied, "the prednisone is helping your inflammation."

Ding! I spontaneously understood the "why" of Beau's prednisone. The steroid controlled the inflammation, the flare-ups. The drug shrunk away Beau's stiff knees.

Dr. Marsh was a rheumatologist, and I had harbored a major misconception about her specialty. It turned out, contrary to my layperson understanding, that she spent extraordinarily little time in rheumatology dealing with arthritis. She didn't deal with old people at all. She spent her valuable time decoding the symptoms of kids like Beau. She made understanding autoimmune diseases her life's work.

Beau was an interesting case, Dr. Marsh explained, because while he exhibited blood abnormalities associated with auto-immune diseases like Lupus, he had none of the typical criteria associated with Lupus and skin. Beau did not have a butterfly rash across his nose and cheeks, and did not have oral ulcers or a rash on any other part of his body – all telltale symptoms of Lupus. Beau also had unexplained bouts of throwing up, a possible symptom of Lupus, but with the long and varied list of possible symptoms, it seemed like turning purple or sneezing rainbows could also be indicative of this mysterious disease.

Once Beau was under the care of Dr. Marsh, one new drug was added to his routine.

Plaquenil became part of the daily regimen. When Dr. Marsh explained that he would probably take the drug for the rest of his life, my eyes rolled back in my head. We were fighting an undefined foe. Beau's symptoms came and went and morphed. His swollen lymph nodes would raise their ugly head for several weeks, and then disappear with no trace. I did not like the idea that at thirteen, Beau might be drug reliant forever. This journey was strange. I could not define a real starting point for Beau, aside from that first visit to the ER, and we had no set destination. We were in free fall.

This random, painful, inconvenient sickness seemed like a transient. We knew it was around. It loitered among Beau's heartbeat. But I, for one, imagined it was temporary. Throughout the weekly blood draws, we had watched Beau's platelet count rebound. The prednisone had taken care of most of his severe joint pain. Without saying the words out loud, I believed, deep down, that Beau's condition was temporary. Someday we would look back on the year Beau turned thirteen with some nostalgia. I imagined we would say things like, "Wow, remember how hard it was for you to walk from the carpool into school?" And Beau, all strapping 6 foot 2 inches of him, would say, in an Arnold Schwarzenegger accent, "Yah, I barely remember; I'm big and strong and strapping now. Yah."

There never was "that day" or even an ah-ha moment when Dr. Marsh came right out and said, "Beau, you have Lupus." Lupus is slimy. It slides in and out of detection. It attacks one part of the body and then retreats; it is undefined. Dr. Marsh subjectively decoded Beau's symptoms as Lupus, and we moved through junior high and high school with the understanding that Beau had an autoimmune disease that acted like Lupus. Unfortunately, we could never plug all of Beau's lab work or vomiting or achiness into a single machine that spit out the words: "Beau has Lupus."

Use of the drug Plaquenil was our biggest indicator as to what Dr. Marsh thought she was treating. Plaquenil is a seventy-year-old malaria drug that is heavily relied upon by Lupus patients and their doctors for the prevention of flare-ups. For lack of a better definition, Lupus flare-ups are the escalation when a patient's own body attacks his joints, eyes, or even vital organs. Plaquenil was a masterful, although temporary, remedy in preventing flare-ups for Beau for years. It worked so well, in fact, that unbeknownst to anyone, Beau ultimately decided to stop taking it.

— 4 —
Batter–Up (or) There's no Quitting in Baseball

The baseball had to go on. "Ms. Casey, he's throwing up again." Quinn, or Quinny-B, delivered this report to me in the bleachers before every game of Beau's baseball season. I cannot believe Beau didn't quit, but Greg was his coach and Quinny-B, Beau's best friend since the first grade in Mrs. Hall's class, was his middle infielder. In between weekly blood draws, physical therapy to strengthen his weakened muscles, and seventh grade homework, Beau stuck with competitive baseball. The life lessons that sports can teach were all amplified for Beau. He vomited before every game but going rounds with Lupus did not break him.

Quinny-B was the only kid in first grade who didn't talk. He wasn't non-verbal in the scheme of autism or being "on the spectrum." Quinny-B simply did not have a word to say in class until he got to sit beside Beau. Something about Beau's mop of shaggy white-blonde hair and big broad smile gave Quinny-B a boost. Quinny-B's pumpkin round face was all chocolate eyes and dimples, and once he was assigned the seat next to Beau, first grade became a breeze for the two of them.

In the beginning, Mrs. Hall would ask Quinny-B to answer

a question, and he would tell the answer to Beau who would then report the answer to their class. One hundred percent of the time, Quinny-B was correct. He could read well before Beau, and Beau could socialize well before Quinny-B. In both looks and in action, one was Ying to the other's Yang.

When the boys turned nine, Greg turned into baseball coach extraordinaire. The three of them rode to and from every practice in Greg's blue Hummer, and by this point in Quinny-B's life, he did not shut up.

"Do you know who the all-time best hitter was for the Red Sox? "Q would ask.

"I'm sure you're gonna tell me." Beau would tease.

"Okay," Q would reply, "tell *me* who is the Rockies fastest pitcher."

The friends would go on like this for thirty minutes. Greg said Q didn't even seem to breathe between listing stats. So, it didn't hit me as too big of a surprise that it was Quinny-B and not Greg, or even Beau himself, who ultimately gave me the vomit reports from the dugout.

In the dugout episodes that Beau endured during that baseball season, there is one thing I regret. Beau asked Greg and me not to share his health crisis with his teammates. He pleaded with us, really, wanting to be a "normal" kid, and we honored that request. However, in honoring Beau's privacy, we stole from him the intense support and camaraderie that a team exists to provide. We also robbed Beau's teammates of the power to pray for, believe in, and genuinely get behind the cause of their teammate. Beau was battling a life-threatening disease. Looking back, everyone missed out on lessons in grace and resilience. For the entire season, except for Quinny-B, Beau's teammates simply thought that Beau threw up before every game because he was nervous.

Lame. I wish I had that decision as a do-over. Calling out the sickness, even labeling the true root of a symptom with its name, does not give that sickness power.

> **Giving sickness a label – different from your name – separates the diagnosis from your identity.**

Calling Beau's sickness Lupus would not have meant he, or any of us, claimed it. Name it. Don't claim it.

I don't advocate using an illness as a crutch or an excuse. A diagnosis is an obstacle, and in hindsight, we should have called it that. Beau's daily fits of throwing up didn't block his ability to be an exceptional catcher, but they did create a detour, one he fought through with the grace of a true champion.

Time after time, game after game, once Quinny-B would report that Beau was throwing up in the dugout trash can, I'd bite my lip with nervous energy, and wait to see if it was Beau who sauntered out as catcher for the first inning or the backup catcher, named Nate. For every game when it was Beau who started – with catcher's gear that doubled his legs in size, and a cowboy sort of saunter any MLB player would be proud of – we had a family victory over disease. These were not just victories for Beau. These were wins for all of us. That spring season, Quinny-B must have leaned his smiling dimples out of those dugout fences fifty times to show me a thumbs-up. Once Beau started an inning, he stopped throwing up.

Greg was present for the boys through three practices a week and tournaments on the weekends. His devotion was without question. The boys loved to tease Greg, and he loved to send signals from the third base dugout to Beau at catcher. During practices, Greg shined.

"I'm just warming up," he would screech, as he pitched screaming warm-ups to his team from the mound.

"You pitch like my Grandpa!" One of his players would yell.

Greg adored the trash talk! His big, muscly shoulders would rumble on the pitcher's mound with the joy of his giggle, which sounded like it came from a ten-year-old. He loved watching Quinny-B stretch for a catch at first base. He loved watching Beau beam line drives toward the third base line from catcher. Greg was thrilled when his team shattered his pitches during warm-up. Week after week for most of the Spring, for every one time Beau and I visited Dr. Shirley for blood draws, he, Greg, and Quinny-B had three visits to the ball field.

Greg joined us just one time for a blood draw. After the initial visit to the ER for Beau's enlarged lymph nodes, Greg tried to steer clear of Beau's medical appointments. They haunted him.

— 5 —
Shock and Loss

Fifteen years earlier, when I was pregnant with Bailey, Greg received an early morning phone call from his brother Ted. Ted, then 23, lived with his parents in the house where Greg and his three siblings grew up. Their mom, a towering woman of nearly six feet, who at the age of fifty-two had the porcelain skin of an eighteen-year-old, had just been rushed by ambulance to the hospital. She had collapsed on the kitchen floor.

Greg and I lived an hour away. Following the urgent call, we threw on our clothes and headed north toward Denver. Halfway between home and the hospital, we stopped at a King Soopers grocery store for a bouquet of roses. We casually talked about which color flowers she'd like the best. When we arrived at the Emergency Room with yellow roses, Greg told the nurse at the front desk that we were there to see his mom, Frances Gent.

Without answering, the nurse stood up and left the desk. Greg turned to me, "That's weird."

We stood there a few minutes longer. I felt baby kicks against my belly and couldn't wait for Frances to hold her hand against them. She and I weren't close. We had nothing in common except for her wonderful son. Now, three years into Greg's and my marriage, this pregnancy had given Frances and I something to talk about. We could fill the typical void of silence by discussing baby name ideas and even the four pregnancies Frances had enjoyed. Babies had been her superpower. I teased that her gigantic man-hands had easily held and nursed and burped her babies. Each of her fingers was a good three quarters of an inch longer than each of mine.

Frances had survived childhood on a desolate farm in Las Cruces, New Mexico. She slept on a dirt floor between several brothers and a younger sister named Evelyn. Frances remembered that her father never spoke a single word. As a teenager, when Greg's dad came to town as a young Army soldier, Frances saw him as a vehicle out of desperation. The two were married within months of their chance meeting; the only thing Frances would miss about home was Evelyn. She wore a wedding band that had been purchased for another woman.

With no further education than a high school diploma, Greg's mom worked for her first fifteen years as a wife and Mother, selling window blinds and furniture reupholstery. She had an eye for exquisite fabric. When Greg and I had just begun dating, I was completely floored by the fact that his mother's couch and living room chairs were completely covered in plastic! There were tiffany lamps on the side tables, pink velvet pillows that had never been touched in the sofa corners, and squeaky plastic-coated furnishings that no one dared sit on for fear of sliding off.

"You grew up in some sort of sitcom." I teased.

"Whenever wearing shorts," he'd whispered back, "avoid sitting on the plastic at all costs. The backs of your thighs won't survive."

The upside to Frances' expensive taste in fabric, was that wealthy families in Denver liked her style. The farm girl from Las

Cruces New Mexico was steadily able to build a successful home decorating business in Denver.

Ultimately, the nurse we originally encountered upon arriving at the hospital never returned to the desk.

"Mr. Gent?" A completely different woman wearing medical scrubs came around the main kiosk and motioned for us to follow her. The yellow roses we'd stopped to buy flopped carelessly against Greg's thigh as we trotted behind the employee; it seemed to be a race chasing her footsteps straight down the hallway and then into a huge room on the left.

When we reached Greg's mom, she lay with her eyes closed and wrinkle-free skin glowing. Greg's dad, brother, and two sisters stood around her like a wreath.

"What's going on?" Greg demanded.

"Mom died." Ted whispered. He spoke without looking up, stroking his mother's soft hand between his fingers.

"No," I thought, "she isn't dead. She is right here! Her face looks beautiful. *Look at her!*" I stared at all of them.

"Wake Up!" I pleaded "Wake Up."

Greg pushed a heart rate monitor out of his way and took his mom's other large hand inside one of his. "She's warm!" he pleaded.

We all stared at Frances. She looked vibrant. Her short platinum hair lay in perfect curls. I fought the urge to shake her.

At 52, Frances Gent was gone, and she lay in death looking beautiful. Greg's mother had died of a pulmonary embolism.

In the room where she died, there was chaos. Medical drawers hung open. The square paddles that doctors must have used to try to shock her back to this world dangled from the bed. It was a horrific, scarring loss. Nurses wandered in and out of the room looking as lost as we all felt. Greg and his siblings took turns cradling her hands. Greg traced his fingertip down each of her long fingers. Greg's dad sat on a hard chair in the corner. We lost track of time. I still don't know how much time we spent with Frances, with her body. Eventually, someone led a line of us out of the room. No one said a word. Greg bowed his head to the floor.

It turns out we all drove our separate cars to the family neighborhood. None of us could go inside the house. We milled around on the sidewalk by the mailbox for more than twenty minutes before I suggested we take a walk around the block.

> **We must have looked like ducklings. Lost. Greg's family had lost its compass.**

For the first few years following his mom's death, the rust-colored sweatshirt Greg had worn the day she died hung untouched on the farthest back hook in the back of our closet. He hadn't reconciled with the sweatshirt or the pain it conjured. He hadn't reconciled with hospitals.

In the first years of Beau's medical journey, Greg could not physically or emotionally make it to more than a handful of Beau's appointments inside a hospital.

— 6 —
His Mother's Hands

I want to live my life aware of miracles. The first tangible miracle in my adult life was the resurrection of Frances Gent. She visited us three years after her death in the form of a neonatal nurse named Norma. Norma was not a miracle-worker. Norma herself was the miracle. It isn't that I can scientifically prove the existence of miracles, or even that I particularly want the words science and miracle to be combined in the same sentence. Despite the debate between my heart and brain, there exists the beautiful fact that I cannot prove miracles *don't* exist. It is this infinite possibility of good things happening that strengthens my resolve for hope on the worst days. There is another fact about miracles that breathes life into my sometimes weary soul: when miracles are involved, no single person gets to decide what defines one.

Nothing about Beau's arrival was normal. I have occasionally held my tongue when friends of mine have shared their glowing delivery stories with women in our circle who are moms-to-be. There was nothing glowing, peaceful, or gentle to share with an expectant mother about Beau's arrival. I was in and out of labor for twelve days.

Beau's due date was May 21, 2000. On March 30, while

rolling a ball back and forth on the living room carpet with two-and-a-half-year-old Bailey, my water broke. The floor was saturated. Bailey thought I piddled in my pants. We both giggled, and in an absurdly calm manner, she and I made our way to the kitchen so that I could tell Greg I was in labor eight weeks too soon.

At the Birthing Center, a nurse confirmed that my water did indeed break. I found it so amusing that anyone besides my toddler might think I was confused about the difference between pee and amniotic fluid. I was pregnant, not two-and-a-half years old.

The year 2000 turned out to be a very good year to go into labor early, and then to somehow hold off the delivery. I remained in the hospital for only two days, mildly hoping that I might go ahead and deliver this baby early and on Greg's birthday, April Fool's Day. When April first came and passed and my contractions were merely a slight inconvenience, my obstetrician allowed me to go home. This was a new era of thinking. Dexamethasone was a drug I had read about for its lifesaving use in climbers above altitude on top of Mt. Everest. It had been injected into each of my thighs each day during my two-day stay at the Birth Center. Doctors believed the dexamethasone would rapidly influence the growth of baby Beau's lungs. For as long as I could carry him, Beau's lungs would be maturing. With four successful injections and counsel to drink electrolyte replenishing drinks or water to renew the leaking amniotic fluid, I went back home on April 2.

The next seven days may be what saved Beau's life. He remained in utero just long enough for the dexamethasone to energize those baby lungs. Sometime around midnight on April 8, with my head resting on the footboard of our bed while Bailey lightly tickled my shoulders and sang, I went into much more drastic labor. I groaned, not from my throat but from my gut.

The second trip we took to the Birth Center was intense. I

was no longer spilling clear amniotic fluid. The leaky fluid was suddenly greenish, which meant baby Beau had made a bowel movement. His vulnerable lungs were now at an even greater risk for infection. Within ten minutes of our arrival, my pubic hair was shaved, and a full epidural was administered. With my lower body now completely numb, a C-section was nearly begun until a last-minute change of plans.

Knowing that baby Beau had received dexamethasone days earlier, my obstetrician decided at the very last minute that those little lungs needed to go through the birth canal to squeeze the amniotic fluid from inside of them out.

Dr. Skiles asked me to push. Fifteen minutes earlier, I had been completely numbed from the waist down. Greg could have pricked a pin into every one of my toes and I would have felt nothing. The instruction was, "*Push!*"

"I think I am. I am pushing, right?" My eyes pleaded with Greg's. I could barely make him out beneath the protective layers of blue scrubs and a mask.

Greg looked at me so intently. "No." Greg said. "Casey, you are not pushing."

This went on for several minutes. Dr. Skiles noted that my futile attempts to push went on for more than twenty minutes before my physical efforts finally began to take effect. With her patience and Greg's encouragement, I delivered Beau at 8:01 am on April 9, 2000. I saw him for one second – his little face and delicate nose were turned toward my right leg – and then someone in the room yelled, "He isn't breathing!"

Four nurses whisked Beau out of the delivery room in their arms. I began throwing up. Greg managed to follow the nurses and our tiny boy out of the delivery room.

The first report came from my father. Beau and Greg were in

the neonatal intensive care unit (NICU). "When you feel ready," he explained, "I can take you down there."

I felt ready.

At age 47, I still call my parents Daddy and Momma. This has never changed. I am the only child born to 17-year-old Debbie Jo and 21-year-old Mark Bradley. My father is 6 feet 2 inches tall, blonde, and fit like a marathon runner. He runs up and down the wooden stairs in my parents' luxurious house sixty times every morning. This is his ritual. He loves fitness and his family. Part of Daddy's beauty is that he intentionally memorizes all our favorites – favorite foods, favorite TV shows, and favorite memories. In recognizing my Momma's simplest pleasure, Daddy keeps a fresh pot of tea steeping on the stove top at all hours. One never knows when his beloved wife of nearly fifty years might want to load up a tall glass of ice and fill it with her mainstay – Daddy's brewed tea. He loves to serve others.

Gingerly, I climbed out of my hospital bed and into Daddy's waiting wheelchair. Neither my Daddy nor I could wait to meet Beau. Neither of us knew what to expect in the NICU. Once Daddy pushed me down the long, pale hospital hallway, Beau's nurse Norma led us through two sets of secure doors into the nursery.

"Your little guy has already amazed us," Norma smiled. "He has extubated himself."

Against the east wall, one in a line of five plastic cradles, lay Beau. His bright eyes gleamed like silver marbles under the light of a warming lamp and Greg's big hand rested on our son's tiny shin.

"Casey, he really did pull the breathing tube right out of his mouth." Greg grinned and looked over at Norma.

After just two hours of breathing help from the ventilator,

Beau's lungs began working on their own. Norma said, "He needs you to feed him."

I had nursed Bailey for eleven months and loved the connection. I assumed that Beau would be a natural nurser, too. Once Norma handed him to me, I smoothed his fuzzy yellow hair with my finger. I also noted that his shoulders were fuzzy. Fine hairs like the ones covering Beau are usually shed before birth, but Beau entered the world before that happened. He was little, furry, and content. Content, it seemed, to not eat. I tried for seven or eight minutes to nurse my precious boy, but he would not latch on.

"Don't worry." Norma encouraged, "We will try again in an hour or two."

I tried to nurse again in an hour. I came back during lunch to nurse. Beau didn't cry or grimace as I have seen brand new babies do. He just lay in my arms, glanced around at the bright lights of the nursery, and firmly pursed his lips closed. This was our routine until dark.

At dinner time, Greg kissed me on top of the head and left the hospital to go spend the evening with Bailey. Bailey hadn't met her brother yet because no children were allowed in the NICU. She had, however, spent an entirely delightful day with my mother. Momma is round and stylish. She wears her hair long, with beautiful reddish blonde waves that fall over her shoulders. This lady who raised me is the greatest reader of *Pippy Longstocking*, the best audience to watch your play, and a belly laugher with no volume control. I didn't worry about how Bailey's Day without Greg and I had been. I knew the wonder of a day with Momma.

Eleven hours old, and Beau still refused to nurse. As I sat rocking him next to his plastic cradle, Norma pulled a chair up alongside mine. In her hand she held a bottle with two ounces of formula.

"Let's get this boy to drinking." Norma gently lifted Beau from my arms, repositioned him, and placed him back into my grasp with his tiny mouth facing my right nipple and legs and feet resting under my right armpit.

"It seems catywampus, doesn't it?" Norma asked. "But it is like you are holding a football, with baby's body tucked in by your elbow. Really tiny babies seem to like being held this way."

Norma readied the bottle of formula and for the first time I noticed her huge, man-sized hands. The slender two and half ounce bottle was completely enveloped by her grasp. Even though Norma was easily thirty years my senior, her hands and face were wrinkle-free. Her skin was lovely, like a rosy-cheeked dolly, and beneath her glasses, she had bluish-grey eyes that seemed to have seen several lifetimes' worth of stories. She didn't strike me as an old soul; she just oozed comfort inside her own skin.

Convincing Beau to nurse took the three of us. While Norma sat next to me, she brushed Beau's lips with her tiny bottle back and forth, over and over, and when he opened his little mouth, I quickly replaced Norma's bottle with my breast. In the dark NICU, with the minimal light of a warming lamp, Norma and I convinced Beau to nurse for three minutes.

"Success!" She announced. "My next shift begins at 7:00 a.m. So, in the mornin', we'll get to work again."

I remember her warmth like yesterday. I remember how she towered over me until she would pull up a chair and sit for our feeding rituals. Twice, she physically grabbed my nipple and held it inside Beau's mouth. She had tricks and techniques. Between bottles of formula and nursing every two hours, this dynamo of a nurse convinced Beau that he liked to eat or, at a minimum, that he liked to feel full. Norma alone was responsible for our six-week premature baby boy leaving the NICU for home after just over forty-eight hours.

Did I remember to thank the angel that helped this happen? I don't remember. But I do have the gratitude and humble appreciation that a seed feels for sunshine and water, because in 2000, for three days and nights, Norma worked with Beau and me on his feeding as if he were her only patient. Saving babies was Norma's superpower. I left the Birth Center feeling Beau had connected with his grandmother Frances Gent.

— 7 —
College Bound

From the time we began treating Beau for Lupus to his high school graduation five years later, Lupus and Beau lived on parallel courses. He didn't have a major episode that involved missing school or staying overnight in the hospital—ever. Lupus seemed somewhat ambivalent. I never dreamed or imagined how dangerous the disease could become. It simply seems impossible to overstate how deeply I was lulled into the misconception that Lupus was nothing more than a name given to symptoms that just didn't fit anywhere else. Lupus did not keep me up at night.

Beau maintained a ritual of Plaquenil and prednisone. There was a short period between middle and high school when he received injections of human growth hormone. Once the season of the aching joints, swollen lymph nodes, and vomiting subsided, Beau simply hadn't grown. At more than fourteen, he was no taller than he had been a year earlier. With the HGH injections, however, he grew three shoe sizes and several inches within six months. Beau was ecstatic.

By high school graduation, Beau was a muscular 166 pounds and 5' 9.5" tall. If Beau worried very much about a Lupus flare-up, he didn't mention it. The onset of achy joints or lethargy that accompany a flare-up in some patients could be thwarted by Beau if he implemented intense naps and intensive sleep therapy. He took one and a half Plaquenil tablets each night before bed, and the drug never failed him.

If Beau started to feel stiff and achy, he would finish high school baseball practice, come home, and fall into bed with his practice jersey still on. Seventeen hours later, he would wake up the following morning by 10:30 a.m. feeling energized. This so rarely happened, that when Beau did need the sleep of an auto-immune-induced coma, Greg and I gladly allowed it. We didn't mind Beau missing an occasional morning class. His grades were superb and attendance, impeccable. He seemed to innately know how to handle the onset of a flare-up, and I genuinely wondered if Beau might just outgrow Lupus.

If Beau's diagnosis ended here, I could have contemplated what we learned the year he turned thirteen and tucked the lessons away. We learned that sickness doesn't define a person. We vowed to live a life of no wasted days. In the early years, our motto just meant showing up for ourselves and showing up for baseball. All the games that Beau survived were a metaphor for hitting the ball out of the park Every. Single. Day.

We realized, too late, that acknowledging his autoimmune disease would not have meant Beau bowed to the sickness. In the future, we would practice calling things what they were. With these bits of wisdom, I might have tied the story up in a neat bow. Finished. Clean. No raw edges. No rough downturns. Beau's history of Lupus would have been shelved. Except that, Beau's character was still to be tested.

My faith was going to be dragged through deep places where the muck gets sticky and heavy and cumbersome, and our appreciation for what gravely ill people endure every day needed polishing. Beau's story with Lupus didn't end here, though it would have been nice.

Greg, Beau, Beck, and I left for Denver and Regis University early one morning, the last Friday morning in August 2018. Beau would be attending the same Jesuit college where Bailey was about to become a senior. Beau easily determined that he would study biology. Bailey studied business and social justice. The mother in me loved that my two big kids planned to live within a ten-minute walk from one another. Even if Beau never took the walk from his dorm to Bailey's condo, I delighted in the idea that he could. Beau straightened his shoulders at the idea of being independent.

"I won't get homesick." Beau told me, after we unpacked his belongings in a steamy dorm room with brick walls and a sliding aluminum window. "There is so much to do here!"

Beau's room overlooked a sprawling green field where students were lounging on blankets and enjoying the sun. We walked around campus, down to the gorgeous green open space, and Beau said "Hello" to everyone we passed. He was in a new element and he owned it.

Continuing the theme of not living a life on hold, Beau jumped into his classes a part-time job at the student rec center. He also started a club for Spike ball, the volleyball-like game that takes the net out of the sky and sets it on a plastic frame eight inches off the ground. Beau never answered my phone calls. For the first two months of college, I got my information about Beau from Bailey. She told me that her friends saw him working at the front desk in the student rec center. I thought he had been so lucky to get a job on campus.

"Also, Mom," Bailey said during one phone call, "I heard that a bunch of girls go lift weights by the front desk, just so they have an excuse to talk to Beau! Little Beauy – all grown up!" She cackled on the other end. Bailey was in gossip heaven giving me the scoop on her little brother.

I missed my big kids in a way that defies words. I wasn't used to the idea of cooking for three or telling the hostesses at restaurants that we were a party of just three. Both big kids being gone at college left me lonely. To make things even more dramatic, Beck started full-day first grade at the same time. Lunchtimes were the loneliest. I missed not having at least two kids in my vehicle at the Sonic drive-up. Grabbing lunch and sitting in the car while Bailey sang Taylor Swift, or Beck *tried* to sing ACDC, just couldn't be replicated. It wasn't until the first week of October, after Beau had been at Regis for more than five weeks, when he finally answered one of my calls.

"Really?" I exclaimed. Finally, his voice was live on the other end. "How are you my buddy? I miss you so much!"

"I'm definitely not bored, Mom." He laughed on the other end. He sounded amazing! "This weekend we're going to Winter Park with a high school group." He told me. "Next weekend we are going to Estes Park."

College life presented Beau with friends who loved the outdoors, friends who loved talking about faith, and a social group who practiced socializing without alcohol.

Beau had a lot to do and very little time to sleep.

"Are you taking any time to catch up on your sleep?" I asked.

"No, Mom. Not really. Tell Beck I love him." Click.

Beau felt so good that he decided to stop taking Plaquenil, and it didn't seem significant to him. It was so insignificant in the scheme of his independent life, that Beau didn't tell me he quit. So many things are possible; maybe Beau experienced the same invincible feeling that a lot of us had as teenagers, or maybe he really believed he had outgrown Lupus. I will always assume that quitting Plaquenil led to Beau's downward spiral. I also don't blame him for testing his invincibility. Sometimes humans need proof that we cannot fly without wings.

Finally, during Thanksgiving break, both big kids came home for the whole entire week. In Bailey's first three years at Regis, she traveled (often over Thanksgiving break) with school groups to El Salvador, the Dominican Republic, Haiti, Uganda, Belize, and Peru. Her once stubborn heart, the one that had grown leaps and bounds of sensitivity upon the arrival of Beck, was now a heart that wanted to serve children in poverty all over the world. Truth be told, with Bailey traveling around the world during her studies and Beau becoming fully engaged in college life, Greg, Beck, and I had literally counted down the days (with bright red check marks on the calendar) until the five of us would be together in our house again!

Thanksgiving week, there was a new addition to our life at home in the forest, and I had been giddy with excitement to share the addition with Beau. In the weeks leading up to the holiday, I finally pursued my lifelong dream of owning a pet reindeer. Like Beau, I lived with the strong belief in no wasted days, and when the opportunity to own a reindeer became real for me, I also operated from a perspective of no wasted dreams.

— 8 —
On, Comet!

From the first moments of my memory, there is my dream of raising reindeer. The rural highway that travels south to north, from Colorado Springs to Denver, lay just half a mile from my childhood home. Momma, Daddy, and I drove the highway regularly to Denver. On either side, for fifty miles, grassland and weathered barns were strewn about recklessly. On this road, in those times, the clock stood still. And on one little brown ranch, west of the highway, there was a muddy colored barn with a grassy pasture that featured a few scattered reindeer. Real reindeer! Their antlers appeared cartoonish and ruggedly heavy from my roadside view. I half believed we might drive by one day and see the top-heavy reindeer toppled over like broken sawhorses. If that happened, I would imagine, the mythical creatures could use their abilities to fly and simply upright themselves right before my eyes. The reindeer along the side of the highway were a dream I never outgrew.

I loved reindeer and their big clunky feet. As a child, I memorized *'Twas the Night Before Christmas,* and gave out photocopies of the text to my extended family members on Christmas Eve so we could each recite a section. My uncle usually rolled his eyes, when I handed him his page, but he one hundred percent participated. The magic of the words "a miniature sleigh and eight tiny reindeer" made me smile every single time. Honestly, nothing about this fascination ever seemed slightly odd. At some stage in my teens, the ranch along the drive that I adored aged out of the reindeer business. Still, every time I rode past, I hoped to see one, and if I were the driver, I'd slow the car down to a crawl just in case reindeer were somehow back inside of the charming pasture. Finally, when all my financial stars aligned the year that Beau left for college, Comet (the very real reindeer) became part of our adventure.

Throughout the United States, only a handful of ranchers raise reindeer. The biggest ranches are in Alaska, but I searched for reindeer in the lower 48 states. Through a reindeer friendly Facebook connection, I made twelve phone calls to different ranches in the hope of purchasing a reindeer calf. Mostly, I was told "No. We're not selling." Or I was given the option to buy two calves, which would have set me back more than $20,000.00. Ultimately, a rancher named Flip accepted my offer to buy one of his bull calves. Greg, Beck, and I took a seven-hour drive to Flip's ranch just a few days before Thanksgiving break, and when we drove into the ranch and past the bumpy cattle guard, Flip greeted us while leading a camel behind him tethered to a leash. I liked Flip immediately.

Reindeer weren't the only unique animals in Flip's ranch. It was dusk, and getting difficult to see across his vast pasture, but we did make out silhouettes of elk, one white buffalo, and zebra. An entire herd of zebra!

"If I had to pick, you know, my favorite?" Flip explained. "I'm real partial to zebras."

Several moms and zebra-fillies (Flip called then cubs) trotted along a corral fence. It felt like the proud moms were parading their cubs for approval, though they didn't make eye contact. Instead, they paraded, tails held high, noses lifted to the sky. Far too noble for anybody's own good.

Flip raised a true bouquet of exotic animals. I longed for more hours in that day.

It had quickly gotten much darker, but in another pen surrounding his massive barn, three or four females pushed each other's necks back and forth trying to get a glimpse of us through a hole in their fence. They were so curious. No pride here. They nearly knocked each other over to get a closer look at the new creatures. Unlike mule deer, or elk, whose noses are shiny black and wet, reindeer noses are velvety soft. Fur covered noses won't freeze in the bitter cold winters like those of their native Alaska or Norway. Those curious reindeer faces peering over the fence looked absolutely huggable. Several of the heifers, or females, looked like they were smiling with big furry lips and no top teeth. I was in love.

Loading a six-month-old reindeer calf into our borrowed horse trailer was, let's say, a new experience. New, in the same way sticking one's tongue to a frozen pole might be considered new. Comet had lived on hundreds of acres of ranchland, and he had never been handled except to receive the required vaccinations. With the moon rising, once Flip got a rope around Comet's neck, he began kicking like a mustang. First, out shot his front legs. When his front legs got tired, out shot his back legs. Greg and I dodged the kicks and his tiny spiky antlers. We were scared. Rescued greyhounds were the largest animals we had ever owned. Nothing about the big docile race dogs had been sharp, but reindeer were sharp in lots of places. Their hoofs are hard. They have dew claws on the back of each ankle, and males and females alike boast impressive antlers. Neither Greg nor I wanted Flip to think we couldn't handle the task of managing Comet, but we couldn't handle the task of handling Comet.

It took nearly twenty-five minutes to move our new reindeer twenty feet from the coral gate to our waiting trailer. Meanwhile, the camel Flip had been leading when we arrived began inhaling the entire bucket of grain that we were planning to feed Comet during the trip home. Misbehaving camels. Bucking reindeer. Greg and I dripped in sweat under our coats, but we closed the trailer door behind Comet. We nodded at each other. Success!

Flip didn't comment on our novice ranching skills, except to demonstrate, on an old heifer named something like Tulip (not Dancer or Vixen) how to stand to the deer's side and reach one arm over her neck and down to a secure hold at the top of the opposite leg. It sounds hard and it was hard.

Heading home made us nervous, and excited. Driving 80 mph through vast miles of Nebraska pastureland also got us a hefty ticket for speeding.

"Po Po got ya real good." Beck teased, giggling in his car seat as Greg pulled the truck and trailer back onto the highway after being stopped. We half wanted to show someone the treasure in our horse trailer, but the sheriff never asked.

"Po Po?" Greg laughed. Beck was hysterical.

"Yep. The Po Po." Beck shrieked.

"A trip we'll never forget." I added.

Aside from Comet, the most exciting site our road trip offered was a collection of wild turkeys.

Following the traffic incident, Beck settled his neck against a cozy fleece blanket and slept for the remaining drive. We arrived home close to one a.m. I stood on the trailer tire and peered between metal slats to see how my new buddy was doing. Comet was laying in the foot-deep straw bed we'd spread along the trailer floor. He even lay wild. His belly didn't touch the straw, making it appear that he could leap from lying to flying in a matter of seconds.

"How's my prettiest boy?" I asked. He snorted.

"Hmmm," I thought, "so reindeer snort."

We were all spent. Greg and I agreed we would each better versions of ourselves come morning. Comet seemed safe for the night in the trailer. The trailer was big enough for six cattle, and Comet could walk around and eat and drink comfortably.

Come morning, my Momma drove into the yard before sunup and peered through the slats of the trailer. I stumbled onto the porch.

"Isn't he pretty?" I asked.

"I love him." She replied. "And his fur is so thick! Will he walk on a lead down to the pasture?"

"He doesn't walk." Greg answered from the open doorway behind me.

"He doesn't walk?" She panicked. Greg grinned.

"He shuffles from side to side and bucks. I wouldn't call it walking."

"He's healthy." I replied. "Don't let Greg worry you."

— 9 —
Dashed Expectations

Our big kids had been listening to me talk about reindeer their entire lives. When Bailey was about nine and Beau was six, we watched a documentary on the Discovery channel repeatedly, almost weekly for several months, because it showed native people in Siberia uncovering Mammoth tusks from the glacial ice. The memory of sharing this video was as fresh in my mind as the frost of that very Fall morning.

Comet had given me a run for my money. For about five days we endured a battle of wills, which Comet won for the most part. Greg and I had only been successful maneuvering him into his newly fenced home pasture by wielding white sheets, Greg on one side and me on the other, to create a tunnel from the trailer to the pasture. Comet had run along our white sheets straight into his new home where pine trees and tall grass were plentiful.

"Now he's up to you." Greg had suggested. He breathed hard. This little creature was a ball of wildness. "I need to get to work."

Watching reindeer pulling sleds of Mammoth tusks in a television documentary had been amazing! In the real world, I hadn't even been able to get close enough to Comet to throw a halter over his nose. I would fill his grain bowl and water bucket each morning, and he would wander in to eat, keeping one eye keenly glued to my movements the entire meal. On the fourth morning, I sat on the ground in Comet's pasture surrounded by pine needles and sent a Facebook message to the reindeer group from my iPhone.

"Do reindeer like treats?" I typed. "If so, I need to bride my calf. Carrots? Apples?" I waited.

"No apples…" came the first reply. "They could be too sweet. My deer love fresh cranberries."

"SOLD." I typed back. "And thank YOU so much!"

If cranberries were a safe treat, I needed cranberries to get to Comet. That evening, I went to the pasture for my supper visit cradling a handful of berries in my left hand and a goat halter in the other. Comet could smell the berries! As I eased through the tall grass in his direction, he slowly inched toward me flaring his big soft nostrils and snorting every third breath. I was ready.

Comet went for the berries, I immediately stepped to his side, wrapped my right arm over his neck and behind his antlers the way Flip had demonstrated, and I pulled the tiny halter over Comet's nose. This was my first chance really to touch him, and he was so soft, like the tufts of a dandelion. His coat must have been an inch and a half thick, I mused. The moment was glorious! Halter half on, Comet began to buck. I stepped away, gathered a breath, and reached around his antlers again. This time, I caught the top of his right leg with my right hand. Then, I moved that hand up to the halter and with both hands and all ten fingers grasping for the buckle, I hooked the halter under Comet's chin. Success!

He shook. I side stepped the pointy antlers. It was a victory. From that moment forward, armed with cranberries and talking sweetly, I made huge strides. First, simply standing next to Comet while I held his halter seemed positive and soon hooking a lead rope to the loop beneath his chin. After day five, I could walk Comet several yards on a lead.

I could not wait for the big kids to arrive home at Thanksgiving and meet my newest buddy. When Bailey and Beau pulled into our drive to start the holiday week, I raced onto the front porch waving and yelling, "Hello!"

Bailey got out of the car first.

"Mom," she said, "it's not good."

"What's not good?" I was puzzled and squinted my eyes. Then Beau stepped out.

"I don't know, Mom. I feel awful." Beau massaged his chest to push away the pain.

My heart sank below my toes. This was not the homecoming I had expected.

Bailey scooped Beck up into a massive bear hug, and he giggled as she carried him away from the porch into the kitchen. Beau and I were left alone in the chilly air.

"Does this feel like a flare-up?" I asked.

He looked at his feet. "Probably."

"Come inside, buddy." I threw my arm around Beau and gave him half the hug I'd been holding onto since we left him in Denver. The way he hung his head on his chest was too familiar. I didn't dare crush him with the idea that these moments felt very similar to his Lupus diagnosis. He lay down on the couch, and I rubbed his feet, praying that if Beau could just catch up on sleep, sleep would fix him. Sleep would fix it all the aching joints, lacking energy, and chest pain.

The first two days the big kids were home, Beau didn't feel well enough to meet Comet. As a professional photographer, I could not wait to stage photo shoots with one of Santa's reindeer. Not only did my own dream come true with Comet, but I could also use him to help kids enjoy real-life magic. During the original fourteen months when Beau was diagnosed with Lupus, I had reflected many times on what made a life worth living. I only ever achieved a partial answer to this riddle, and my answer continually circled around the belief that people only come to regret the things they do *not* do. So, I did become a reindeer rancher. As much as I enjoyed Comet's soft nose and the sniffing, he did of my pockets filled with cranberries, Beau did not feel well enough when he got home to leave the couch. I wanted Comet to sniff Beau's pockets, but my buddy didn't have the energy. We asked him to call his rheumatologist and he did.

For me, there was this transition between Beau being a child patient and becoming an adult patient, which felt like I was learning to drive a stick shift all over again. It was herkie jerky in every way possible, and it had to happen during the only week that Beau was home from college. When his phone call was patched through to Dr. Marsh, I fed Beau the questions I wanted his doctor to address. I had the life experience to be my child's advocate, but he was nearing nineteen and living independently. It was imperative that I renew his desire to get well –not merely to survive until the next Younglife weekend getaway. I have to scoff at myself for the lofty goals I set for that one quick Thanksgiving holiday, but I intended to heal Beau fully, train him as a self-advocate, and fulfill Bailey and Beck's vision of a magical family reunion within five days. Also, I wanted everyone to love Comet.

Dr. Marsh understood Beau's urgency. I assumed she must appreciate how rarely Beau had reached out to her over his high school years. She prescribed a prescription strength pain medicine for the heaviness in his chest, and she increased his daily intake of prednisone. Beau slept the entire Wednesday before Thanksgiving, and by evening, he rallied enough for a game of Pictionary. It wasn't much of a rally. Bailey and Beck were making their own Thanksgiving memories. We baked brownies and painted wooden ornaments for the Christmas tree. I was grateful, almost content with the sense of fun that swirled inside the walls of our cozy home, but I wasn't giddy. Throughout most of Monday, Tuesday, and Wednesday, Beau was missing from our memory making. He laid on the couch while I worried.

Thanksgiving morning brought Beau a tiny spark of energy. The high point of the day, for me, was that Beau did walk outside to meet Comet.

He's just a little guy," Beau said, surprised.

"Yep. He was born in May." I answered proudly. Comet shook his tiny spiky antlers, and Beau slid cautiously closer to the fence.

"Come on, Buddy," I chided. "He is just a baby."

A healthy Beau would have lingered with us among the trees and earned our new pet's trust. Instead, Beau headed gingerly back inside. He wasn't good. He moved like an old man.

Upon heading back to Denver after the holiday, Dr. Marsh asked Beau to stop by Children's Hospital and get his blood drawn. She would check the Lupus markers. Beau fought through aching joints and the heaviness in his chest to finish out the fall semester. He renewed his commitment to Plaquenil, but his mind couldn't seem to relay the message to his Lupus.

— 10 —
Lupus Hits Hard

By February, Beau was hospitalized for the first time due to Lupus. He'd withstood six years of a diagnosis and six years with no hospital stays. On Valentine's Day 2019, every former Lupus success came crashing down. The transient disease I once imagined disappearing was back with enormous effects. My adult son's autoimmune disease was creating autoantibodies. Dr. Marsh called the marker "anti-double stranded DNA." She knew enough about Lupus to understand that the presence of double stranded DNA meant Beau's disease might be mounting an attack on his kidneys. Beau had dealt with joint pain. He had endured long bouts of daily vomiting, and the heaviness of inflamed lungs and a painful chest. Quite dramatically, Lupus was affecting an entirely different part of Beau's biology.

As a result of the Lupus flare-up that began in November, Beau's blood markers had gotten progressively worse. Dr. Marsh worried about Beau's creatinine marker, a number that I learned represents almost everything there is to know about the general health of a patient's kidneys. Between November and February, his creatinine marker jumped from 0 to 3.1. By doing an online search, I discovered most college-aged young men have a creatinine level between 0 and .09.

Dr. Marsh gently reminded us that she was neither a nephrologist nor a kidney specialist, but at our first family appointment since Beau had gone to college, she explained in simple terms that Beau needed a kidney biopsy. It would show a cross section of what was going on inside his body. The biopsy would be taken from his left kidney, which is customary, and a nephrologist assigned to the case would look for scarring in the sampled tissue.

Greg and I had walked alongside Beau's gurney, as he was pushed toward the surgical room where he would be sedated while a surgeon inserted a long, slender needle through his back and into his left kidney in order to grab a sample piece of kidney tissue. Once we entered the sterile room, I assumed that Beau had to be one of the biggest kids being treated at a Children's Hospital. I started to ask that very question, when suddenly, as the anesthesiologist and surgery techs took steps to move Beau from one gurney onto his stomach on a second gurney, there was a loud pop. Bang! I jumped, and the new table under Beau collapsed. It all happened so quickly, but as Beau fell, Greg caught him. One of the nurses screamed. I screamed. It looked like the legs of the gurney were never locked.

"Mom," Beau mumbled, "I'm fine." He lay precariously in Greg's massive arms. Beau was not shaking, but I was. I took half of Beau's weight and cradled it against me. Every activity in the room paused for the next several moments.

"Greg caught Beau." I kept repeating inside myself. Greg was the only human in the room who had reacted quickly enough to save him. Beau now lay in our arms. The two of us held Beau upright while the doctor and her helpers secured the collapsed table. Moments before the heart-stopping thud, Beau had been given a sedative. Standing there now, holding my man-child tightly against my body, it struck me as impossibly cruel that as the table was collapsing, his own reflexes were medically inhibited. Beau – athletic, quick, and wiry – was too drugged to react. Gravity pulled him. I felt mad. I felt bitter. Once again, tears poured down my cheeks.

"Do you guys work on children the size of Beau very often?" I offered my question up to the room. It had started as a simple thought, but now my words took on the drama of the past five or six minutes. What I was really asking was, "Are you people – you in the masks and scrubs – physically capable of being entrusted with my 18-year-old child?"

"Absolutely, Mrs. Gent." The anesthesiologist ignored the words of my question and answered what I asked between the lines. "We will keep three people around the sides of the table the entire time Beau is here. He won't be able to roll anywhere."

Greg double and triple checked that the surgical table was secure. He literally bent at the waist and shook each connection. Beau relaxed as the breathing mask was fitted over his nose. He closed his eyes, and we were asked to step outside for the sterile procedure. We did not know what Beau's kidney biopsy might reveal. Results from the blood tests Dr. Marsh had been running concerned her, and she was hard to rattle.

Beau had lived with Lupus for six years, and this was his first hospitalization. One point for the good side. The fact that his kidney numbers were only newly elevated also gave me hope; point two, fingers crossed. Maybe Dr. Marsh had caught the increase in Beau's creatinine levels so early that quick intervention would heal Beau's kidneys. Creatinine was a term we were hearing over and over in our talks with Dr. Marsh. It was the main marker related to Beau's kidney function, and without a biopsy, the only proof that Beau's kidneys might be in trouble.

I couldn't wrap my head around how innocent and sweet and lanky he looked when Greg and I met back up with him in the recovery area of the hospital. He was encouraged to lie flat on his back for one hour following the procedure. Once he heard my voice from behind the curtain, he began waving his hand in the air and calling to us.

"Hi guys! I'm in here!" Beau called. For the moment, he seemed seven and not nineteen. "I am having the *best* slushy." He smiled, still flat on his back. His sweetness melted me.

"Beau is the happiest patient I've seen wake up today." His bedside nurse giggled.

Beau had a joyful response to sedation. His hospital stay following the biopsy consisted of three days where he received one prednisone infusion of 1,000 milligrams each day. This was well beyond the scope of the 10 milligram prednisone tablets that helped Beau's symptoms so quickly in the beginning. I suddenly had the shifting perspective of a mother thinking, "Maybe prednisone really *is* what the medical profession throws at anything they cannot decipher." One side effect of these huge hospital infusions was that Beau tossed and turned at night. He rolled, sat up stick-straight, lay down and rolled to the other side. Repeatedly.

I slept on a squeaky plastic couch beside him but realized Beau didn't sleep or even rest. Throughout each night he worked diligently on homework. Beau controlled what he could – his studies. The trajectory of his disease was now on an entirely different course. We would find out the next path in Beau's Lupus journey while on vacation.

— 11 —
No Wasted Days

Our family of five gathered around an outdoor breakfast table, where the splash of waves crashing over a short sea wall was almost deafening in the sleepy town of Kona, Hawaii.

Eight days earlier, Greg and I had sat in the waiting room of Children's Hospital while Beau underwent his first kidney biopsy. Sitting together in Hawaii for a family spring break trip was ten million times better than sitting in the hospital. We had been told to expect that sometime during our vacation; a nephrologist would call Beau with the results of his kidney biopsy.

Aside from looking slightly swollen and puffy, Beau seemed like himself. At our breakfast table in Kona, the plate of pancakes I had ordered appeared in front of me, though I didn't see our waitress serve it. Bailey noticed helium birthday balloons in the waitress station along with a shot glass of whiskey. It was 9 a.m. and our waitress was drunk. Today, it seemed, was her twenty-first birthday. Each of these unusual factors made the morning all the more jumbled in my head. Was it early or was it late? Why did I order pancakes instead of something healthy? When my phone rang with an unrecognized number, I hadn't answered. When the same number rang Beau's cell phone, he picked up.

"Mom," he said. "It's Dr. Gieger, the nephrologist. He wants to talk with you."

My face turned hot. I felt wobbly. "This wasn't good," I thought.

Beau was an adult. Dr. Gieger could have just talked to Beau, right? Waves crashed over the lava wall. Our drunken waitress laughed loudly and hugged a familiar customer.

I took Beau's phone.

"This is Casey."

"Mrs. Gent? Dr. Gieger here. We got back the results of Beau's kidney biopsy."

"Yes," I replied. Each of my feet shook nervously under the table.

"I am disappointed to tell you, "The doctor finished, "that Beau is in the fourth stage of kidney failure."

Wait. What? Hadn't we caught Lupus attacking his kidneys early in the game? There are only five stages of kidney failure, and I recalled briefly reading that treating stage 4 was considered the most challenging. The morning continued to seem surreal.

"Okay." I answered. Somehow, I managed to reply calmly. "Do we need to fly home?"

"No. No. Enjoy your time in Hawaii. We will meet when you get home. We will make a treatment plan for Beau."

"Well, do we have time for that?" I prodded. "Can this wait for a week?"

Dr. Gieger, in his gentle Austrian accent, assured me that one week in the care of Beau's kidneys would be insignificant. "I'll see you guys next week," he finished.

I clicked the off button on Beau's phone and handed it back

across the table. Beau looked at me pleadingly. His face was puffier than I had realized, but I didn't know enough to understand that his body was not doing its job. His kidneys were failing to filter the toxins out of his body. Beau was puffy with high blood pressure and water.

"So," I searched carefully for the right words. "The doctor says you do have *some* kidney failure."

"What stage?" Beau asked.

"Four." I answered.

"Mom, that's not *some* kidney failure. Four is bad. Like, the worst." Beau stood up and asked Beck if he wanted to walk around together in front of the restaurant. Before Greg or I could reply, Beau had Beck on his shoulders and the two were headed out to the ocean.

My sweet husband of twenty-five years leaned gently across the table and whispered, "Is stage 4 really that bad?"

"It is." When we saw Dr. Marsh last, she gave Beau and I each a colorful graph depicting the stages of kidney disease. Stage 4 was labeled as "Moderate to Severe kidney damage." I grabbed Greg's hot hand and felt it trembling like my shaky knees. It was a weird sensation to be in paradise and feel so profoundly sad.

In the ten minutes that it took for us to leave the restaurant, Beau returned with his brother, lifted Beck off his shoulders, and asserted, "No wasted days." This was his call to charge forward with our plans for the day in Hawaii. It also meant we would talk no more about his kidneys for the rest of the morning.

I don't think anyone can really prepare themselves for a bad diagnosis. I don't think anyone *should* prepare themselves for a bad diagnosis. If human beings can rise up to meet the best of their thoughts, which I believe we are, then the best energy of thought must teeter on the side of hope. Always, we must set our thoughts and our moods on hope. When hope fails, it is a perilous, sinking, and desperate fall, but our thoughts cannot lie with the fall. Hope must rise. Our thoughts must rise.

I do not believe it serves any worthwhile purpose to let a grave medical diagnosis – a worst case medical diagnosis – indefinitely define a family's spirit. Just how long can we wallow in the fall of hope? Long enough to catch our breath. For me, after hearing that Beau was in the fourth stage of kidney failure, that involved an afternoon nap, completely shutting off my mouth, and asking God "Why?"

Each time we hit a diagnosis with Beau that was graver than the one before it, I experienced four recognizable stages (for me) of coping.

1. **Shock.** In this phase I feel my heart rate escalate, I have an upset stomach, and race to the toilet with diarrhea, and regardless of where I am, I cry.

2. **Re-Group.** In this phase, a day after the shock, I revisit what the doctor has said. I reach out to my friends and parents and ask them for prayer. I remind myself that we are a unit; neither Beau nor I will deal with this diagnosis alone.

3. **Re-Plan.** In this phase, I email the doctor with a call to action. Is there a new med to try?
   Are there new therapies? Should we consult with specialists outside of this hospital? Where do we go from here?

4. **Renew Hope.** In this phase, I allow my faith in a God that is good to over-rule my brain. I think about the fact that I am fearful, but not hopeless. With

God's strength inside of us, we are never fighting
alone. There is fear in hope, but also light. I physically
look at Beau and see that he is breathing, and we
are functioning one day at a time. I believe in good
things happening, and I tell Beau that he is loved.

At the same time Beau's kidneys were failing, candidates for
the 2020 presidential election began to campaign. When I didn't
want to read about kidney disease, I read about the candidates.
In my 25 years of professional photography, I had photographed
candidate Clinton and candidate Obama. The political stage
fascinated me, and it was particularly fitting when Cory Booker
shared a quote on Instagram that I latched onto immediately:
"Despair never gets the final say." On my left forearm, I carry a
tattooed quote from Mother Theresa which reads: "Kind words.
Endless Echo." This is an abridged version of her beautiful truth
that said, "Kind words may be short and easy to speak, but their
echo is truly endless." I could see that sometime in my future of
tattoos, Cory Booker's quote would occupy my right wrist:

| **Despair never gets the final say.**

— 12 —
Big Symptoms and Bigger Feelings

Several mornings into our island vacation, Beau's swollen ankles and puffy cheeks began to take a toll on his upbeat attitude. The five of us huddled around another outdoor breakfast cafe, and baby chicks scurried in and out around our toes. This was paradise for me. Country and farm life exuded from the pores of each island town we visited, and I had to refrain from bending down to pick up the tiny chicks. Dang, were they loud! The proud hen and rooster looked on from ten feet away, cautiously pecking at waffle scraps thrown to the ground for the fluffy babies. Beau ordered only toast, and he didn't touch it.

"My chest is really heavy." Beau explained. Then his lip quivered, and a tear rolled away from his eye. Then, poignantly, he finished by saying, "I don't want to live like this."

"Oh, of course you want to live!" I countered back.

"Yes, Mom," he lifted his head that rested on his heavy chest and rolled his eyes. "Of course, I want to be alive. But not like this."

Beau motioned his hand toward his feet, prompting me to look at the fact that he wasn't able to slide his flip flops over the doughy swollen top of his foot. His ankle bones were also not visible behind puffy, rash-covered skin. He labored to breathe and generally exhibited from the outside what it must be like on the *inside* of a body at war with itself.

"My knees hurt. My whole body is puffed up. I feel bloated even when I don't eat..."

Beau cleared his throat but continued crying.

"I'm so sorry, buddy." Greg said. He grabbed Beau's hand across the table. Greg was magnificent about listening without trying to fix everything. We could not fix this. Not yet.

After shooing the chicks away from underfoot, we loaded back into our rental jeep. Beau plugged his iPhone into the radio, dialed up the volume, and played a popular song from the album *Father of the Bride* by the band Vampire Weekend. None of us was talking. Bailey held Beck's hand in the backseat. Beau tucked himself inside the grey hood of his sweatshirt and closed his eyes. The family mood was melancholy. I listened intently to the lyrics of the song Beau was playing. They were about anger wanting a voice, problems that won't go away, and a desire not to live like that, but also not wanting to die.

— 13 —
The Slow Plan

When we got back to Denver, I would be deeply understating our situation to say that getting an appointment for Beau with Dr. Gieger was difficult. For three straight days, I could not get anyone at the clinic to even call me back. Then, the entire state of Colorado began to prepare for an impending blizzard. It wasn't a surprise snowstorm, but an "Albuquerque low" that weather forecasters had predicted many days ahead. On day four, when Dr. Gieger's nurse did return my calls, she tentatively said, "I don't suppose Beau wants to wait and be seen after the bomb cyclone?"

"No." I interrupted. "Did you happen to see that Beau's kidney biopsy showed him in Stage 4 kidney failure? Stage 4. I do not care about the bomb cyclone."

"I did see that," she answered sheepishly. "Let's schedule a conference call with you and Beau and Dr. Gieger during Thursday's storm."

It was not ideal. "Not ideal" was a phrase I came to use often in my feelings about the treatments and results during Beau's battle with kidney failure. Seeing Dr. Gieger in person would have been much better, but a phone appointment meant we were on our way to a plan of action. When we first started a treatment scenario with Dr. Gieger, Beau had a creatinine level of 3.1. Not only do kidneys produce urine, but also they filter the body's blood. When they work, kidneys are to the body what catfish are to the lake. Kidneys clean the passageways and filter out the gunk.

The average healthy individual sitting next to you at Starbucks or on the bus likely has a creatinine level between .05 and .09. Initially, I did not feel panicked by Beau's creatinine level of 3.1. But when we finally did get a chance to talk with Dr. Gieger, he explained that the concern with the number was that prior to Beau's Lupus flare-up around Thanksgiving, he had a consistent creatinine level of .07.

"We are concerned about the increase. We don't like any increase in this marker," Dr. Gieger explained, "so we have to get the creatinine stable."

Outside my window, it was snowing sideways. I hated it when the forecasters were right about big storms. Mostly, I hated it because their accuracy inevitably kept me *in*. Nine days earlier, when Bailey, Beau, Greg, Beck, and I had arrived home at the airport following our trip to Hawaii, Beau had been adamant about returning to college. Why, he argued, should he sit complacently at home when he could remain studying at Regis which, by the way, was only fifteen minutes from Children's Hospital? Greg and I agreed. This plan of action followed right in line with a) not living a life on hold and b) no wasted days.

From his phone line at college, Beau asked, "How are we going to keep the creatinine from climbing?"

"We are going to hit it with prednisone and another drug called Cellcept." Dr. Gieger answered.

"Prednisone," I thought, "our old frenemy."

After one week, when treating a simple virus or bacterial infection, prednisone has done its job of energizing the patient and defeating the sickness. Regarding kidney failure, prednisone can be used for months and years. Side effects of the drug, for Beau, included an inability to sleep, swelling in his face and occasional blurred vision.

"Beau," Dr. Gieger finished, "We are going to have to see you in the hospital two times this week and two times next week. You will be getting infusions of prednisone. What days do you have class?" Dr. Gieger's heavy accent lent his pronunciation of Beau to sound more like "Boh." It was endearing.

The two agreed on Tuesday and Thursday prednisone infusions, and I planned to drive up to the hospital from Colorado Springs to sit with Beau during the two and a half hour treatments. Though not ideal, I was really glad we were taking action.

Two weeks later, Beau and I sat in the glass-enclosed infusion room at Children's Hospital. From our stories-high vantage point, we could see the city of Aurora sprawling out and turning green the farther our gaze went, and to the west was a view of the Rocky Mountains that led our eyes into infinite layers of blue. If we had been there for any other reason, I am certain we would have profoundly appreciated the sunshine and surrounding architecture. Hospital designers, I reasoned, had spent a lot of energy making this structure feel less like a hospital and more like a hotel. I loved the fact that even when Beau was an in-patient, he was never asked to wear a hospital gown. Children and young adult patients were encouraged to wear sweats and comfortable clothes, items that felt like home. The attention was placed on getting better, not on being sick.

On this visit, the third of four scheduled prednisone infusions, Beau's evolving disease rammed him head-on into a brick wall. The labs that were drawn after each of the previous week's infusions were discouraging. Even with the intervention of intense steroid therapy, Beau's creatinine continued to climb. In our earliest conversations with Dr. Gieger, he had emphasized that to shutter Beau's kidney damage, we had to stabilize the creatinine. For the time being, nephrologists throughout the world followed a basic set of steps to stop Lupus nephritis (Lupus attacking the kidneys). For Beau, if step one was ineffective, his treatment would climb to step two, then step three, and so on. Dr. Gieger's approach wasn't revolutionary. I read of nearly identical steps being followed to treat Lupus nephritis at The Mayo Clinic. This realization both soothed and agitated the Momma in me. Beau's treatment plan was rather unremarkable but also well tested. I began to fear the final step of kidney failure, which in my mind, meant dialysis.

I mostly denied myself thoughts about dialysis. On the rare occasion that I did think about it, the mental image instantly appeared of an old, yellowed man, wrinkled by sickness and discolored by disease, as he sat attached to a grungy silver dialysis machine in a rundown strip mall. The image reeked of hopelessness and despair and yet, in a painful twist, it also embodied an old man who had at least already experienced one gift that Beau was fighting for –his youth.

Once we could see Beau's creatinine continuing to climb, even with the huge infusions of steroids, I called Dr. Gieger to ask privately if Beau was looking at dialysis. I stood among tufts of sprouting green grass with Comet, feeding him handfuls of cranberries, and allowing salty tears to streak my face. Reaching out to Beau's doctors was usually exhausting, and ingesting painful news seemed more tolerable when I was outside. On that day, like one or two times before when I had asked Dr. Geiger how close or far Beau was from dialysis, Dr. Gieger answered, "He does not need dialysis." But this time he added the kicker, "We need to start thinking about chemotherapy."

This is not cancer! I did not believe we were now contemplating chemotherapy for a non-cancerous autoimmune disease.

I wanted to put on the brakes, to yell "Stop this ride!" Our family seemed to be speeding down a medical path for which we weren't prepared. I hadn't packed. I hadn't done enough research. During our November visit to Children's Hospital, Beau and I were sitting with Dr. Marsh talking about chest pain and Lupus. Six months later, Beau and I were making weekly trips to Children's for steroid infusions, and now I was on the phone with Dr. Geiger discussing kidney failure and chemotherapy. We were all over the map. This journey could not be charted. Beau's medical diagnosis seemed to have no starting point and no destination.

Today, I look back in wonder at why we jumped onboard with chemotherapy, but my realization is this: We never had the chance to unload. With a grave diagnosis, the path changes, the conductor switches hats, and there simply isn't the luxury to stop.

— 14 —
A Heavy Realization

Beau was not prepared to discuss banking his sperm – not at eighteen, not as a college freshman, and not sitting next to his mom. But as we sat contemplating the use of chemotherapy to stop Beau's body from attacking itself, the fertility specialist for Children's hospital made her way into the room. I hadn't expected that a children's hospital would need an expert in fertility, but there she was. There was a great deal more *unexpected* about Beau's diagnosis than we could ever have planned.

After introducing herself as Dr. Shandy, the fertility specialist settled right into the generous cushioned chair next to Beau. In the way she sat, so comfortable, deep and molded into the chair, I got the quick impression she had not taken the load off her feet in 100 miles. She also was not even slightly uncomfortable about using the terms "sperm" or "ejaculation." Minutes into her arrival, Dr. Shandy easily controlled the room.

"If you start chemotherapy in two days (which was Dr. Gieger's suggestion)," she explained, "You will be taking a very low dose of chemo." Dr. Shandy detailed that Beau's chemotherapy protocol would include six infusions, and the infusions would each be spread about ten days apart.

"I just don't know if the amount of chemo you will get is enough to kill off all of your sperm."

Beau's eyes became massive, round. He did not look child-like; it wasn't the look of embarrassment or discomfort. There was no squirming in his chair as he sat with prednisone dripping steadily into his IV. It was like Beau's wide eyes and motion-less lips reflected a problem so huge that he could not physically or mentally wrap himself around it. His expression was heavy, sad, and disjointed. Nothing in my life had prepared me for this depth of low. This unplanned conversation was a revelation: After enduring all the steps it would take to save Beau's kidneys, not one thing would ever be the same.

"Have you thought about having children in the future?" Dr. Shandy wondered. If so, she wanted Beau to understand that the time to bank and save his sperm for the future was, well, imme-diate. He basically had two days.

I tried piecing together the words my teenager couldn't find. It seemed like I was thrown under a cloak so heavy with sorrow, I might never shake it.

> **There was profound sadness in my sick teenager being faced with questions surrounding his own mortality.**

Asking Beau to see beyond his current medical journey, or even beyond his freshman biology class, was like asking him to leap headlong into a dry pool. In the question about whether or not Beau wanted to be a dad, there was no safe answer. It simply felt like going down a black hole. But we both immediately felt the familiar and purposeful gift of our youngest, Beck – a gift I still could not fathom being lucky enough to receive.

"Beau's little brother is adopted," I began. "In fact, each of my older kids has talked about wanting to adopt."

Ah ha! Maybe I could make this doctor understand that family for us was not about biology. Did I want her to understand that Beau would not be defined by his fertility? Maybe. Did I want her to know, mostly, that we were not prepared for this conversation? Absolutely. Finally, was Dr. Shandy right to give Beau options? Even options that were not ideal? Yes.

"Yeah, I'm not too worried today about banking my sperm." Beau declared. "Hopefully I'll find a wife who loves adoption as much as *we* do."

At the word *we*, Beau turned his glance in my direction. His eyelashes brushed the top of his cheek, and he suddenly smiled with so much warmth and wisdom and exhaustion that it crushed me. His blue eyes had evolved from wide to distant to peaceful – in a snap. We loved adoption. We did! And it felt like a weight was lifted.

"Okay then," Dr. Shandy replied. She stood up to leave, content with Beau's decision, but added, "And remember, we just do not know. It is possible you may one day father a child biologically."

— 15 —
Back Where We Started

We had not entered the heavy white door on the second floor of the cancer center for six long years. Beau and I were back in the Cancer and Blood Disorders Clinic of Children's Hospital, and queasiness moved over me. So many years had passed. Beau was now different in every way physically, from his deep voice to his hairy man legs and 5-foot 9-inch stature. Bringing Beau back to this place was a painful retreat into a battle I thought we'd won. This was a failure. But Beau would not quit. He, Greg, and I had agreed that if low doses of chemotherapy were the next best step in saving his kidneys, we wanted to remain on track and take the next best step.

Just inside the heavy metal door, Sherry, a familiar receptionist, greeted Beau as if no time had passed.

"I'd remember you anywhere, Mr. Beau," Sherry smiled. "You're a whole lot taller, but you've still got that million-dollar smile." I noticed she was only seeing Beau's half-attempt at a smile. He studied the ground, fiddled with the medical bracelet she'd just handed him, and tried to avoid further small talk. Beau turned his back to Sherry's desk and looked out the window.

"Sherry, it's wonderful you're still here!" I chimed in. I smiled warmly, because seeing one face that we saw years before really was slightly comforting.

If Beau were younger, I might have chided him for being impolite. Let's be honest, I would have definitely told him he had to do better. But at this point, I realized, as the mother of a perpetual patient, that the toll of constant medical appointments was heavy. It just was! There was so much redundancy to the receptionists, techs, nurses, and doctors, and at every single appointment, my child longed to be anywhere else – anywhere but there.

I came to see Beau's half-smiles and short greetings as a way for him to protect the essence of Beau. Chronically ill kids simply cannot pour their energy into *every* medical professional who gets interjected into their story. Rudeness is never acceptable from any patient, but as Beau had less and less energy for small talk, I came to see his short interactions as a healthy boundary. In the simple, quick answers and half-smiles, Beau retained some power. Whether he knew it or not, this was Beau protecting his soul. Beau's gift for clever conversation, and his massive toothy grins that showed every tooth –both bottom and top – were not gone. They were preserved.

After finishing a few pieces of paperwork, the two of us were situated in a gloomy room with no window and a disappointing nurse explaining how Beau's vein had simply "disappeared" underneath her second IV stick. I hated this moment and all the others like it when Beau had to get stuck more than one time. To me, it didn't matter if he was getting a simple blood draw for labs or an IV start. I wanted the nurse to do her job the first time!

Beau's initial chemo infusion was one needle stick away from not happening.

Four or five minutes after the two unsuccessful attempts at starting Beau's IV, the charge nurse joined us.

"Why," I asked, "hadn't we been given her expertise from the beginning?"

"It's okay, Mom," Beau winced. "I think she will be able to get it. It's no problem."

"Thank you, Beau," she grinned. "I'm Heather." Heather did get the IV started in one stick. She warmed his arm with a heating pad, laid his arm out across her lap, and did her job.

"In the future, if you don't have me as your nurse," Heather explained, "please tell whomever you *do have* that your veins roll."

Heather got Beau's real smile. He and I also latched onto her bit of advice about the rolling veins. I figured I would throw that tidbit out there to any of Beau's future nurses who might listen.

Before starting Beau's chemo infusion, Heather put on a paper coat, paper pants, and a disposable splash guard covering her face. I had heard about chemo for what seemed like most of my life, but I had not imagined what it physically meant to infuse toxic chemicals. Outside all her protective layers, Heather held the chemo. Inside an IV bag sloshed a liquid that looked like water, and at several spots on the surrounding bag were labels marked "Poison." The chemo bag was only a couple of inches full. Heather held it away from her body like a dead mouse. Then, attaching the bag so it dripped slowly into Beau's IV, she set the timer for an hour. Beau said his mouth immediately tasted like aluminum and asked for gum. He felt nauseous, and then mercifully, he fell asleep.

Chemo was more than one IV bag. There were additional liquids to infuse that protected Beau's bladder, and some that insured he was not dehydrated. The process took seven and a half hours. Beau was nauseous on and off. He tried to eat. He did sleep. We had visitors too, which eased the monotony, including my best friend Sarah, whom I had met at the Tri Delta sorority house in college. Sarah was present for all my life's biggest events.

In a glittering emerald, green gown in 1994, Sarah was the maid of honor at my wedding. Three years later, she changed Bailey's first diaper, cried tears of joy as she agreed to be Beau's godmother in 2000, and sat with me, rubbing my shoulders at Beau's first chemo appointment. Every Momma needs a Sarah.

At the end of Beau's first chemo infusion, around 4:00 p.m., nurse Heather unplugged Beau's blood pressure monitor, took a last record of his temperature, removed his chemo IV, and sent us packing with a few granola bars. Beau drug his feet to the elevator. He did not say anything. I wondered if chemo had been what he had expected. He said he had zero expectations. When we got to the car, we sat momentarily in silence. I thought about people who survived. People who survived chemo, and mothers like me who wished they could take their child's place. We sat. It felt heavy. We both took deep, long breaths. Beau let me hold his hand for an instant.

"Where would you like to go now?" I asked. "Does a smoothie sound good? Or an apple?"

"I want to get an ax." He answered.

I turned my head sharply and laughed at him.

"An ax?" I repeated. I laughed loudly and my gut shook and some of the heaviness lifted. I had to blink hard twice before I could stop.

"Why an ax?" I asked. "I meant; do you need something to eat?"

"An ax," he answered, "because there's tomorrow."

Reaching across the console between our seats, I squeezed Beau's knee. Of course, there was tomorrow, and an Ace Hardware near home to stop and buy his ax, and trees in the forest to trim, and kidneys inside my boy to save.

— 16 —
The Fighter's Spirit

Handling the up-and-down lab results from Beau being sick threatened to shut me down.

Beau seemed able to compartmentalize the bad news. He never put away the fact that his kidneys were failing, and he created a small section in his mind allowed to worry. The remainder of his mind was left wide open. So, an ax. Beau rarely lived in the despair of a moment.

We received weekly updates from Dr. Gieger regarding Beau's blood work. None of the updates were good. Dr. Gieger always called in the early evenings when I was outside with Comet.

I would rub my reindeer's soft fur, and all the while, my eyes would stream tears under the evening light.

Beau's creatinine was climbing, his double-stranded DNA was high (which was a bad thing), and Beau retained so much water that he had developed a beer belly. It exhausted me. My body wanted to sleep away the bad. Without Comet to walk and sweet Beck, who constantly wanted to build Legos or go for hikes, I would have never left my bed. Beau, however, did leave his bed and even the walls that enclosed him.

On the days when Beau had enough energy left after chemo,

he wanted to drink in the fresh air. He would walk out the kitchen door with the new ax dragging behind in his left hand. Our eight acres of property in the Colorado forest was awash with pine trees; they stretched every direction for as far as one could see. Beau would stake out a tree, one not too far from the house, and begin trimming the lowest branches. I would see him step away from the tree and study it to the top. Beau was always in awe of nature. What I learned from him was this: control the moments you do have and live them with intention.

Beau's outside moments lasted no more than 15 minutes. After chopping ten or fifteen branches, Beau would lean against his ax, or sit on a log, and then rise up and knock a few big branches off again. I'd feel physically amazed by his tenacity. His legs were like tree trunks themselves, with no definition between his ankles and calves, not even a dimple marked his knee joints. Beau stood on these thick, waterlogged stilts with shrinking shoulders and a bulging belly. His silhouette looked nothing like the Beau I knew.

Prednisone was failing. Chemo was failing. An additional drug caused Beau so much nausea and diarrhea that the treatment was worse than the disease. I decided we needed to think outside the box. Beau said he was up for alternative care. We agreed on acupuncture.

— 17 —
Alternative Medicine

"You're really sick," Dr. Chang looked Beau over. He poked his finger into Beau's swollen ankle, and it left a doughy, half-inch indentation. Dr. Chang was one of the city's most well-respected acupuncturists, and when I initially called to make Beau's appointment, it amazed me Dr. Chang himself answered the telephone. He was a one-man show.

Fifteen minutes prior to Beau's exam, the waiting room in Dr. Chang's small office hosted a rotating parade of loyal patients waiting for appointments and new patients picking up "Chinese medicine." The stream of faces was young and old. One woman walked with an exaggerated limp, while other patients looked fit and well from the outside. Beau and I agreed that the number of people inside the office must mean Dr. Chang was helping some. Maybe he was a master decoder. We spoke to a woman seated next to us who said that before she started seeing Dr. Chang, she had been unable to walk because of arthritis.

"Look at me today!" She grinned, practically leaping out of her chair to show off her newfound mobility. "He gives me pills." She explained. "I don't know what the hell they are, but they're definitely working. I've only been coming here for six months, and I can walk again."

Was she proof? I simply did not know what to make of this one-stop Chinese pharmacy/acupuncture clinic. I did know that modern medicine, for my child, wasn't working. Since Beau had been home from college for the summer, he had endured prednisone infusions and started chemotherapy. I had watched him get progressively sicker. Fighting the urge to flee, we stayed in the acupuncture office. Shortly, we had our turn.

Beau lay on a comfortable cushioned table in the back of Dr. Chang's office. There was a thin wall and an intricate screen separating him from the reception room. As quickly as I blinked, the doctor had tapped six miniscule needles into Beau's protruding stomach. Then he made his way down Beau's body and tapped several additional needles into each of Beau's ankles. The ankles immediately began to leak water. Under each needle, water oozed from Beau's legs. He was absolutely drowning in liquid.

"Does it hurt?" I asked.

"No." Beau answered. He shrugged his shoulders. "Not at all."

"It's your kidney and your liver." Dr. Chang explained with certainty. While Beau lay flat, the doctor dropped five tiny black pills into Beau's cupped hand. The pills looked like shiny onyx pearls – completely round and exceptionally smooth.

"Take these." Dr. Chang insisted. He handed Beau a cup of warm water.

"What are they?" I asked.

The doctor answered, "Chinese medicine."

Beau and I exchanged glances. Tiny needles stood like soldiers all the way down Beau's stomach to his feet. Before he had enough time to talk himself out of it, Beau threw the tablets to the back of his throat and washed them down with a decisive gulp. With that, we were invested.

Dr. Change required $500 for a two-week supply of black pills, tea powder to mix with water, and six acupuncture visits that would occur sometime within the next twelve days. Greg had sent us with a check for $250. I cleared my savings account of cash before our arrival, and with $500 paid, Beau left Dr. Chang's office feeling "slightly better." Once inside the car, Beau handed me his collection of new medicines and pills. The bottles were labeled in Chinese. I had no idea what Beau would be ingesting. Part of me was utterly shocked at my behavior, at my willingness to proceed on this completely random path.

You should be disgusted with yourself, I thought. The FDA has no idea these pills are even inside the USA! But more of me was desperate than disgusted. Desperation – and an ounce of hope – won.

Beau invested himself in Dr. Chang's regimen. He took the pearl sized pills religiously and went to his acupuncture visits several times a week. After two weeks, Beau still carried more water in his heavy legs than he had the weeks before. Stretch marks began to cut deep purple canyons in his stomach and along his back, and I felt like the unconventional treatments were a waste of money and energy. The stretch marks were a product of water and waste overcoming Beau's failing kidneys. His body simply lacked a filter, and his skin stretched painfully to hold the excess weight. Two of Beau's stretch marks were more than half an inch thick – deep purple and tender. While some patients experience kidney failure over a period of years or decades, Beau experienced a relative shutdown of his own kidneys in a matter of several months.

We continued to see Dr. Gieger and Dr. Marsh. It wasn't that we eschewed conventional medicine, but we were certainly looking to improve it.

Beau continued to get weekly lab draws, where sometimes he was poked once but usually twice, and his creatine pushed 5.0. Creatinine levels between 9.0 and 11.0 mark complete kidney failure.

I texted my very sweet friend Tracy, that "Prayers for Beau didn't seem to be working." She had offered to add Beau to her prayer chain, and in a particularly flawed moment, of which I am not proud, I followed up with another real zinger that read, "God probably isn't real anyway."

Yep, that's what I typed, and in the moment, I didn't feel even sheepishly sorry. It was easy to be angry at God.

Two days later, Beau was admitted to Children's Hospital again. It was a few days before my birthday. I worried if I had jinxed my son by texting my friend that my faith was failing. Beau was well enough to walk into the hospital. He had a skyrocketing fever, a blood pressure rate of 167 over 92, when he did pee (which was rare) his urine created foam inside the toilet bowl, and he was vomiting on and off. The foamy urine was another sign of sick kidneys. We watched another young man, Beau's age, wheel himself in alongside us. His feet were deformed – unable to reach the ground from his seated position – and his head sat askew at the top of his spine. As he rolled his eyes from side to side, he smiled broadly.

> **I could not rationalize where my God was for the kids who were sicker than Beau, for the ones who didn't get better.**

I never assumed a patient could not get better. No person has the right to extinguish all hope, but the patient beside us, confined to a wheelchair forever, would not be getting well.

However, visiting hospitals and clinics with Beau had led me to understand there were levels and degrees of being well. The state of wellness is a bunch of lab numbers and symptoms, but wellness also correlates with human relationships. The young man who wheeled his crippled body into the hospital next to us didn't flash that huge smile because he felt particularly *well*, but inside the hospital, he had formed relationships that connected him to life. Connections offered a piece of joy and a shot at hope.

Standing in the airy hospital corridor, I felt keenly aware of the sick children and their families who moved in and out around me. The hospital offered cheery red wagons for sick kids to be ferried around in, and wagons of kids were scattered everywhere. Were children being healed? I wondered. Children were being diagnosed, but were children healing?

Doctors diagnosed hard, almost unthinkable illnesses. As a parent, I felt like I was handed a choice between two sides of a coin. On one side, there were sick children. So many sick children, in fact, that a massive hospital was required in Aurora, Colorado just to serve a few of them. This side of the coin was heavy, and I was burdened by the idea that if there were a God, how could God let children get sick?

On the other side of the coin, there were healers and miracles. This side of the coin was light. It was carried by the idea that because there is a God, healers and helpers develop the will and knowledge to make children better.

To anyone who has felt like God isn't listening, or like they have been abandoned, don't be too hard on yourself. Doubt is more rational than faith.

In the hardest moments, if you, like me, have just one friend offering to add you to a prayer chain, or one doctor seeing you regularly because he or she has not given up the fight, then you must look to those faces and those relationships as your glimpse of something bigger. These faces are the tangible proof of faith.

Choose the light side of the coin and have faith that God is inside of the helpers and the healers. For each sick child in Children's Hospital, there were more than a dozen medical professionals who came to serve them. I could see God's goodness was alive.

Once Beau settled into his room on the sixth floor, a nurse named Madison gently popped her head in from the hall and said, "Hello!" She asked Beau his pain level on a scale of 1 to 10, with 10 being almost unbearable.

"I'd say a 4 or a 5," Beau answered.

"Okay," Madison replied. "What is your goal for pain control today?"

My immediate thought was, "*Madison, his pain goal for today is 0 – duh!*"

However, Beau's answer surprised me. "I'd be okay with a 2 or a 3." He replied. His answer was eye-opening on two levels. It revealed that Beau lived in some degree of pain every day, and yet again, he revealed that wellness, tolerance, and survivability are each completely subjective.

During this hospital visit, Beau was transferred out of the care of Dr. Geiger.

He had been a sort of wait-and-see doctor. Dr. Geiger had hoped the prednisone infusions and chemotherapy would stop Beau's body from assaulting his own kidneys. Heck, we had all hoped and prayed for that type of resolution! But four months into the journey of kidney failure, we were now looking at a young man with maybe 10 percent kidney function.

There are five stages of Lupus nephritis. A kidney biopsy gives a nephrologist the absolute best view "inside" his or her patient's kidney. The long, slender sample of tissue, removed by a surgeon while the patient is totally sedated, shows both current kidney inflammation and the scarring or damage that has already happened. Scarring is a long-term problem. While I learned about Beau's disappearing kidney function, I came to see the scarring in his kidneys like ocean coral. While hardened and dead coral maintains its shape, it serves no purpose in the ocean. Beau's kidneys were taking up space, but they weren't doing their job.

During this hospital visit, Beau was placed under the care of five nephrologists from the kidney team at Children's Hospital. In the nephrology clinic at Children's, it appeared that three nephrologists specialized in pre-transplant care and two focused on post-transplant care. The on-call doctor this visit was named Dr. Saprano. Long brown ringlets fell along her face and her brown eyes were pools of warmth. She was ridiculously excited about kidneys, which correlated with her being ridiculously good at explaining kidney lingo. A smiling, purple kidney-shaped emoji dangled from Dr. Saprano's stethoscope. She was well versed on Beau's medical chart, and although his previous kidney biopsy was only four months old, she ordered a second one.

"Obviously, I'm disappointed you're back in the hospital." Dr. Saprano stated. "And it's certainly not your fault, Beau." She smiled, sorrow on the edge her lips. "We need to see inside. How much more have Beau's kidneys been damaged?"

He had endured four months of prednisone, immunosuppressive drugs, chemotherapy infusions, and droves of high blood pressure medicine.

"What's another biopsy?" Beau shrugged and grinned.

As I stood across the room from Dr. Saprano, with one hand resting against Beau's bed, I feared we were heading toward dialysis.

There are two types of dialysis. Hemodialysis and peritoneal dialysis. Peritoneal dialysis can often be performed at home, because it involves circulating a cleansing fluid through a catheter in the patient's abdomen. Beau's bloated stomach was so pronounced that this type of dialysis was immediately off the table for him. Hemodialysis, the more plausible option, purifies the blood of people who are in kidney failure. It removes creatinine and excess water from the blood. After Dr. Saprano explained the process, I knew Beau's swollen body desperately needed purification. Hemodialysis almost always takes place in a dialysis center, with nurses and techs who are trained to use the filtration machines.

"Beau will need a port." The doctor drew a breath and looked at her feet. She continued,

"The surgeon will insert a line somewhere just under Beau's collarbone. The line will tie into his heart." Dr. Saprano locked her delicate brown eyes on Beau. "What you'll see, every day, is about three inches of plastic poking out from under your skin."

Plastic tubing? Another biopsy? I felt wrecked, lower than the floor. I started to explain that just before Beau's *first* kidney biopsy, he was practically dropped off the table. I started to speak. I wanted to advocate, and I could not. Instead, the deepest, ugliest cry I have ever uttered found its way outside of myself.

Beau lay between Greg and me and the doctor. His lean shoulders shrank away from his bloated belly. In the corners of blue, where his eyes used to glisten, was flat grey. A second biopsy? A surgical line straight to Beau's heart?

"I," exhale, "cannot breathe." I explained. "I can't breathe."

Beau looked to Greg, both absolutely stunned. I was not keeping it together. My sweet buddy, tethered to his bed with an IV line, tenderly stared at me with his mouth wide open and his eyelids fluttering. He looked, for one breath, like crying.

I cried. I cried for all of us. I cried for so much failure. By this point my lower back leaned heavily against the windowsill. One hand was on each hip. I stood like I was recovering from a race.

"Oh Beau," I sobbed. "I just don't want them to drop you."

And beyond that, I did not want dialysis, or the three-inch plastic tube, or the failed kidneys. Where was the rewind? The reset? Dr. Saprano brushed past the foot of Beau's bed and hugged me hard. For at least one minute, she hugged me without letting go.

"Oh Momma, you were obviously traumatized by Beau's last biopsy." She acknowledged.

"Obviously." Beau whispered.

> **Doc widened her stance and stood with one hand on my shoulder and the other on the foot of Beau's bed. "With all the power I have," she promised, "I will not allow the team to drop Beau."**

— 18 —
Dialysis

When Beau awoke from the second biopsy, there were a few similarities to his first kidney biopsy and one very big difference. This time, just beneath Beau's collarbone, on his right side, was a very precise hole with several inches of tubing that stuck out. Just out of surgery, Beau was wrapped in warm blankets, and I could not see it. For at least three hours following a kidney biopsy, the patient is required to lie flat. Because of this precaution, Beau also could not see his port, but I only imagined. There must be blood. I wrung my fingers. I envisioned being able to see underneath Beau's skin.

Convenient, I thought, *I need God again.* I also imagined God could probably take it – my anger, my frustration, my pleas for help sitting inside of my own skin the first time I looked at Beau's port.

Greg and I accompanied Beau and his gurney from surgery to the hospital dialysis center.

"How do you feel, sweetie?" I asked.

"I actually feel pretty good." Beau turned his head to his right and smiled at me; then he winced. "Felt that." Beau blinked and took a breath. "That must be the port."

I walked several steps ahead of Beau's gurney, trying to calm my heart. There we were. Dialysis. Along the journey of my son's kidney failure, I had feared this result more than any other. In my lengthy strides through the corridors toward the dialysis unit – and between my deep, anxious breaths – I felt a marked shift in Beau's care. Several months earlier, we were trying to save Beau's kidneys. Today, we were trying to save Beau's life.

We had built no momentum in the direction of healing. It felt like Beau's diagnosis was changing and moving so fast yet going nowhere.

If I traveled this path again, I would have weekly conversations with my child's doctor about the end goal. Were we all headed to the same place?

Inside of the dialysis unit at Children's Hospital, there was a lot of sunshine. One full wall of glass shone natural light into the airy space that looked nothing like the dirty strip mall dialysis in my imagination. Just five patients could be treated in this unit at once. I expected it to feel like a kidney failure factory, and it was nothing like that.

With Beau still lying flat on his back, a dialysis nurse introduced herself and gently peeled away the blankets covering Beau's port. There it was. I had to look, and I wanted to.

"It's very clean." I explained to Beau, surprised. A tiny bit of blood had dried on Beau's chest, but the port itself was not gory. There was a clear tube coming out of the lifesaver-sized hole in Beau's skin, and his nurse put on a face mask and surgical gloves before she touched it. While handing face masks to Beau, Greg, and me, she explained that any time the tube was open to the air, everyone in the surrounding area must wear a mask.

"We want to keep the port more than clean." She smiled. "We want to keep it sterile."

Then, for thirty seconds, the nurse wiped and re-wiped

Beau's tube with alcohol. I watched her follow the second hand on the large wall clock as thirty seconds slowly passed. Finally, she attached his embedded tube to an additional line of tubing leading into the dialysis machine. This machine was named Aladdin. It was about two and half feet wide and four feet tall, but most of the work looked like it was done in a cylinder on the front. I liked that. For a second, dialysis didn't seem so serious. But once the filtering started, and we watched Beau's blood leave the port in his chest and enter the dialysis machine, things got real. I watched my baby's blood leave his body, be cleaned in the oblong filter at the front of the dialysis machine and re-enter his system through the clear catheter in his pale chest.

> **I felt panic. I wanted to flee, to go outside and release my anxiety, but my feet stuck. I stuck. Greg stuck.**

"Does it hurt?" Greg asked.

No answer.

"How you doing, buddy?" I asked.

He closed his eyes and nodded up and down. I took it to mean he was surviving. Together, for the moment, each of us was surviving. We made it through a one-hour treatment and the first dialysis experience. His nurse explained that once he was able to stand up and walk into dialysis, he would weigh himself upon arrival and prior to leaving. Slowly, assuredly, dialysis would remove the water weight collected in Beau's ankles and belly. As his gurney was wheeled back out of the dialysis unit to his hospital room, Beau said, "It wasn't that bad."

"When will Beau be able to get the catheter wet?" I asked. By day's end, his nurse was preparing us to check out of the hospital, and we needed a few details finalized.

"He won't." She answered. Beau and I attempted a laugh.

"Seriously, though, he needs a shower."

"These types of ports cannot get wet. At all." The nurse explained. She wasn't joking.

Baths, normal showers, a quick dip in the pool or a hot tub, even water gun battles with Beck – all of this was now untouchable. A vision of Beau leaping into the waves on our last trip to Kona flashed before me. Dialysis didn't just steal activities Beau loved, it also stole the decency of a warm shower and the freedom of going shirtless on hot summer afternoons. Dialysis was a thief that gave life. We would despise it and rely upon it both at once.

Before heading home, Beau was given a "Roo." The Roo was a fleece sleeve, no more than three inches long and an inch and a half wide. It served as a sort of sock for the end of Beau's catheter. I thought the invention was a brilliant way to keep the tubing from catching on his clothes. If only it worked to wick away water.

— 19 —
Staying the Course

The first week that followed the insertion of Beau's catheter was ugly.

It was midsummer, which meant the days were sticky. Sticky, even in bone-dry Colorado. Beau couldn't stand to have any clothing rub against his tube let alone rest on or stick to it. I bought three double extra-large T-shirts. These were the only three shirts Beau touched. After three days, Greg hurried the roomy T-shirts into the laundry and sanitized them for another three days. Beau walked around the kitchen and the living room with his shoulders hunching forward, his tube pushed out against the baggy T-shirts. He wore knee high compression socks to help his swollen feet and legs. My teenager moved like a geriatric patient.

When he sat on the couch, Beau covered his port with an armor of pillows so that our two sweet lap dogs wouldn't accidentally jump anywhere near his tube. One of the Dogs, Brooks, was a rescued Chihuahua with a saintly spirit. For every minute Beau lay or sat against the couch, Brooks lay with him, fur touching flesh. The skin where the port entered Beau's chest remained raw and slightly red. Beau was exhausted. I would drive him from home to dialysis at Children's Hospital twice a week, and during the hour-long drive to the hospital and back home again, he slept in a daze. He was surviving, and in some degree of pain, constantly. Beau merely existed between dialysis treatments. In this life, in Beau's life, we wanted far better than survival.

Then after we were ten or twelve days into dialysis, Beau stayed awake just long enough during one of our car rides home from the hospital to talk about the classes he planned to register for during Fall semester. We had hope, a glimmer of looking toward the future, and then, just as suddenly, an infection.

At 8:00 a.m., day 16 with a port, Beau had walked into the hospital under his own power for his scheduled dialysis. By 10:00 a.m., he had such intense abdominal pain that he could not speak. The on-call nephrology doctor immediately checked Beau into the hospital where he had to be moved by wheelchair to his assigned room. He lay against the bed sheets with a pale, almost blue cast to his skin. He took big, heavy breaths that he labored to blow out of his body. There was great confusion among the hospitalists, the doctors on Beau's floor of the hospital, as to why my child's temperature kept climbing. At 3:00 p.m., I raced down the hallway outside of Beau's room and grabbed his attending physician by the arm.

"We are missing something," I pleaded. "I understand you are giving Beau one antibiotic through IV, but it isn't touching his symptoms."

"We're actually giving him two antibiotics in that drip line," she countered. "His blood work just isn't growing anything yet."

I took this to mean they were looking for an infection and couldn't find one. All the symptoms of infection were present. Shortly, an infectious disease specialist entered Beau's room. Beau was either asleep or trying to be. Every few moments he groaned but was too weak to readjust himself. It was nearly dark, and Beau now had two nurses assigned specifically to his care.

"Has your son traveled out of the country within the last month?" The infectious disease doctor hit me with a laundry list of questions. "Has he been near caves or anywhere bats are present?"

"No, and No," I answered. I did offer that Beau's sister had recently been working with children in Singapore.

"Probably not problematic." She replied.

With one eye on Beau, I alternately tried decoding Beau's symptoms with each of the specialists assigned to him. We all agreed that Beau's body was fighting an infection, but neither the source nor the location of it could be determined. The dialysis nurses had carefully swabbed Beau's port just before he was admitted. Five or so hours later, that culture had grown nothing. I finally asked the on-call doctor how often a patient presents an infection that can't be found.

"All the time." He answered. He shook his head from side to side, because science wants a target. Doctors want something more than an invisible enemy. In his next breath, Beau's doctor said to expect that my son would be moving to the Pediatric Intensive Care Unit (PICU) within the night.

Greg had just reached the hospital. I leaned into him and lay my head beneath his scruffy chin. Greg's work clothes wore a light sheet of sawdust and his face was marked with dirt form the jobsite. Beau acknowledged his dad with a nod of the head.

"I don't want to expect that we're moving to the PICU. And actually," I continued, "his temperature is not climbing at the moment."

Beau was far too sick for both of us to step outside of the room to talk, so we talked and stood by the side of the bed.

"What are you hoping the doctors do?" Greg whispered.

"Well," I replied, "I am not as concerned about the source of the infection. Right now, we just need to hit his body with everything we can to fight."

With Greg in the room, I headed back into the hallway to find Beau's attending doctor.

"Is there another antibiotic?" I asked.

The doctor followed me back into Beau's room and felt Beau's abdomen. It remained pliable, which was good, but Beau could not stand being touched. When I asked if his pain level was near 10, he nodded his head yes. But with his abdomen remaining soft and his fever not continuing to spike, the doctor said there might be a third antibiotic they could try. He left the room and called the infectious disease specialist for a third time. The infectious disease doctor wanted X-rays.

When multiple specialties are working with a patient in Children's Hospital, opinions are collected, gathered, and weighed within "the team." Beau's team had one doctor on the floor who communicated the team's philosophy with me. Throughout the late afternoon, communication was getting lost in the shuffle between the team and the on-floor physician. Beau had not been allowed to eat or drink since we were admitted. His mouth and lips were dry. By dark, when the on-floor doctor came in to explain that Beau was going to X-ray, I shared my frustration. I knew the very best doctors were those who weren't threatened by questions. While knowledge is power for all people, knowledge is peace for the momma of a desperately sick child.

"Here's what the team thinks," the doctor began, "one consideration is that Beau's stomach has developed little leaks, and that those leaks have seeped into the peritoneal lining.

The X-rays will prove or disprove this idea."

He gave me credit for understanding, and I felt better just having some idea of Beau's symptoms laid out before us. I heard about the peritoneal lining, weeks earlier, from Beau's acupuncturist, who also thought all the water weight in Beau's stomach was impacting his liver. My understanding was that the peritoneal lining was a wall around Beau's abdomen. Each of us was decoding the clues that Beau's body revealed. Could an infected sac around Beau's stomach be the source of sepsis?

"If there are leaks," the doctor concluded, "we cannot introduce food or water. That's why we aren't allowing Beau liquids or food. But here's the good news: little leaks can disappear in 24 hours."

Getting Beau to X-ray was a monumental task. Just after 10:00 p.m., two nurses, Greg, and I wheeled Beau's bed through the darkened hallways of the hospital. For me, everything that's hard is harder at night. The absence of light blankets my thoughts with intense hopelessness. I longed for the sun, even when it would be blue at dawn before it was warm and golden, and I wished the sun would hurry.

The long hospital hallways felt like passageways. Each time Greg maneuvered the bulky bed around a corner, Beau moaned. I held his hand. It was almost the size of his daddy's hand. It was a grown man's hand, and his long, pale fingers lay limp in my grasp. It was the first time I feared I was losing my child.

Once In the radiation room, a tech asked Beau if he could scoot from his bed onto the table. I could see Beau try to gather a big breath. Either his throat or lungs failed in the process. The breath didn't happen. He could not move from his bed to the table.

Greg was shifting in his work boots. He took his hands in and out of his pockets. He looked at the wall, then the floor and, ultimately, standing helplessly next to our child was not good enough. My gentle husband, with his massive hulking shoulders, stepped back up to Beau's bedside and lifted our 19-year-old child like a baby bird. Wet tears streamed down Beau's cheeks. He cried the tears of a soldier – making almost no noise but unleashing unbearable grief in the streaks that ran along his face. Greg's feet were shoulder-width apart. Beau lay across his forearms. I turned my head, gulping hard. The image I saw was wilted and desperate. I hated it and I loved it. Greg was everything to all of us.

There we stood. No time to wonder why. Greg held Beau, who was folded in half, shaking, teeth chattering as he fought his fever. We needed just three X-rays, three quick pictures of Beau's abdomen. It was impossibly hard to watch. The minutes were long and slow on the clock above the X-ray table. I gritted my teeth with the desire to crawl inside of Beau's body and bear his pain. Greg held Beau for the three X-rays. There was caked mud on the floor beneath his boots. Beau's bare legs and feet dangled limply from Greg's strong hold.

Afterward, enough time had passed for more IV pain medication. It neared midnight, and the on-floor doctor reported that he had gotten approval to start a third antibiotic.

"That's wonderful." I replied. "Wait, why in the world," I wondered, "did I say *wonderful?*"

Nothing was wonderful. Greg, who had worked a full day before racing up to Denver, was instantly asleep, sitting fully upright against the plastic cushions beneath Beau's hospital window. I had placed a cool cloth on Beau's forehead, and for the first time in my bank of memories, Beau asked me not to rub him – not his forehead, or his shoulders, not his hands, ankles, or feet. He could not stand to be touched. Even a bedsheet was too heavy on his stomach. Down the hallway, my own momma was resting in a vinyl recliner. Each time she had walked into the room, she turned around and left, sobbing.

"Good to see they haven't moved him." One of Beau's two nurses stepped lightly into the room. About thirty minutes had passed since all of us had taken the trip to Xray. I stopped thinking about everything that was bad as I glanced up.

"Maybe Beau won't be moving to the PICU tonight," she whispered. "Fingers crossed. Also, I have the new medication."

At that moment, one thing was good: Beau was not declining. I knew I had to stay awake. I pulled a folding chair up to the bedside. I took my socks off and left both feet bare, touching the cold floor. I needed just enough discomfort to stay awake. My hand rested on the rail just next to Beau's arm. He could not take anything orally, so an IV of the antibiotic began to drip. Drip. Drip. Forty minutes later, we got a glimmer of hope. Beau's fever dropped below 101 degrees.

For the next four hours, I watched Beau sleep.

He seemed to be breathing with less effort. Maybe? I wasn't convinced, but as the blue light of dawn trickled into the hospital window, I realized we had made it through the night outside of the PICU.

By 9:00 that morning, Beau had the energy to talk.

"Mom," he said. "I'm done. I can't do this anymore."

"You're not done," I answered. "There are all kinds of great things the world needs you to do."

I wanted him to take it all back – his words and his wrecked spirit. I looked at his swollen face, pumped full of steroids. In my glance, I caught another glimpse of the IVs I had studied throughout the night. He was bruised from an IV that had already blown. He was exhausted, worn out. But I knew we weren't done.

"We've been here before." I said, running my hand through his shaggy hair. He didn't brush me off. I grabbed my phone and found the picture of Beau at thirteen, fragile and weary but not broken.

Beau gently took my phone and studied the photo.

"I'm done." He repeated.

This time it didn't sound so sharp.

Our second day in the hospital started with the familiar collections of blood and samples from around Beau's port. The team was still looking for the source of infection. I am hesitant to say we all wanted one of the samples to grow something. An answer, a scientific cause for this infection such as bacteria in Beau's blood or around his port would make the case of his septic infection open and shut. By 4:00 p.m., none of the samples collected from either day had grown anything. The team wanted Beau to undergo another procedure.

"He has been sedated three times in the last two months," I argued. "Two biopsies, six infusions, chemotherapy, and the insertion of a port for dialysis." I raised my voice but wasn't yelling. "No. Beau will not have another procedure."

Beau's team of doctors were reacting as scientists. The procedure they suggested involved gathering samples of the peritoneal fluid surrounding Beau's stomach. He would have had to endure anesthesia again and the danger of having his belly probed by a long needle.Beau was improving. I just could not imagine subjecting him to anything further that day. In the back of my brain, I saw the future – a future with transplant surgeries and intense healing. But first, we had to get him there.

I asked the nephrologist: "Would the results of another procedure change anything about the way you are treating Beau's infection?" I asked.

"No."

"So, why pursue additional testing, when, regardless of the results, the antibiotics used to fight said infection won't be changed."

No one patted me on the back that day or said, "Good job, you stood up for your son!"

But I felt empowered. Regardless of how sick Beau became, and his team all agreed that Beau was fighting sepsis, our family retained a voice in his care. This voice felt important. The doctors wanted more scientific data from the peritoneal lining, but the data would be just data, and that was where humanity had to prevail over science.

By evening, Beau was allowed to eat dinner. Once he took a turn for the better, it was simply stunning how quickly he improved. Beau stayed two more nights in the hospital, because two of his infection-fighting antibiotics had to run their course intravenously. Each morning, blood samples were drawn from his IVs and from his port, and each evening we were told that none of his samples had grown a bacterium. This would be one of those cases where an infection existed, and its source could not be completely explained. In Beau's series of three X-rays from his first night in the hospital, no leaks were visible in his abdomen. While the doctors wrung their hands, frustrated by not defining the source of Beau's sepsis, our family became more thankful by the hour as Beau's symptoms slowly improved.

The morning Beau was set to be released, I left Greg with him in the hospital room and went for a run. A crisscrossing band of concrete trails wind around Children's hospital connecting the grassy front area to the university hospital on the neighboring block. This set of trails proved life-giving to me during the moments when I simply had to be outside. Butterflies and bees dodged between fragrant bushes. An enormous number of bunnies lounged in the grass. Occasionally, if it was sunny and pleasantly warm, I'd pass other parents pushing their children in wheelchairs or pulling them along the paths in a red hospital wagon. These moments in the fresh air were the good ones, but how I wished, later, that I had ears in the walls for the conversation Greg had with Beau while I was gone.

Understandably, Beau had become blah. He was mentally and physically droopy. He didn't hold his head straight and hadn't pulled a brush through his hair for the entire stay. Greg couldn't take it. We agreed our first son was becoming a shadow of the great design life had in store for him. But I didn't have the guts to say it to Beau. I couldn't form the words out loud that he had to care again.

Who was I, who were we, to ask our child to do any more than simply survive? Yet who were we to watch him fade into a sketch of himself? Thankfully, while I ran, Greg managed to totally amp himself up. Tough love wasn't a normal part of our parenting, but on the morning of Beau's release it seemed like Beau's spirit needed shaking. Greg and I had agreed, from day one of parenting, that the world would knock down our kiddos often enough; that it was our job to lift them up. However, once Beau said the words *"I'm done"* we were fighting a different sort of battle. Everything was at stake.

"I don't see how you are going to go back to college in a few weeks." Greg had said.

Beau was propped up on pillows looking at the list of books that were required for his fall classes. He thrived at college with his people.

Evidently, he replied to Greg, stunned, "Dad, I have to go back."

The two stared into the space between them. Beau didn't blink. Then Greg, our soft and steady family rock, asked, "Do you have what it takes to go back?"

"Absolutely." Beau had answered. "No doubt." Greg said our

son sat straighter. At this part in the retelling, the skin on my forearms lifted lightly with goose bumps.

"I think you have what it takes," Greg had encouraged, "but you said you're done?"

"I want to go back." Beau replied. "I'm going back. My friends are there."

Greg shared that Beau's voice shook, but our boy had his fight back.

I grabbed Greg's rough hand and wiped my forehead; still sweating from my earlier run.

"Good job, Daddy," I told him.

"You know, that's all I wanted," Greg explained, smiling at me with aqua eyes that began to drip. "I wanted Beau to fight for his spirit."

When we checked out of the hospital, there were two weeks left before the end of summer break.

A nutritionist on the nephrology team had ordered kidney shakes for Beau, and they arrived in big heavy boxes on our front porch almost immediately. He had butter pecan and vanilla to choose between. Nepro shakes are specifically designed for dialysis patients and are low in potassium and phosphorus.

Beau seemed stronger after a couple days of drinking the shakes. He packed them in the back of his van.

Ten days later, with all signs of infection gone and dialysis effectively keeping Beau upright, he headed back to Regis for the start of his sophomore year. Each of us refused to let his life be placed on-hold. On-hold wasn't living. Studying, Spike Ball, the library, friends, professors, and independent living had to be given more attention than the role of dialysis. Dialysis was one part of Beau's life, but we gave priority to an attitude of no wasted days.

Beau looked frail in his button-down blue shirt. Beck hugged him gingerly for a goodbye photo. They both had fresh haircuts, because it was part of our back-to-school tradition, and I thought some things just needed to feel normal.

> **"Fake it 'til you make it," Greg said to Beau. Intention and purpose. Beau wasn't really ours anymore to let go, but we supported him flying again.**

"Remember, humans need wings to fly." I said this inside myself and texted Beau not to be late to dialysis and not to stop taking Plaquenil. Ever.

— 20 —
The Weight of The Weary

I was traumatized by so many health scares so quickly. On a completely unremarkable

Wednesday mid-Fall, I took Beck to school, came home, and immediately got back into bed. I pulled our fuzzy oversized teal comforter tightly underneath my chin and closed my eyes.

"This isn't normal," I thought inside myself. "There are portraits to edit in the studio.

The dogs would love to go for a run." Still, I lay there, hiding.

My mind knew what my body *should* be doing on a typical weekday morning, but did my mind also know that I was not the one in the family in kidney failure? It seemed I was living too close to Beau's pain. My heightened sense of worry lulled my brain into thinking that maybe my body was the one that was sick. As I lay beneath the covers, one full and precious hour ticked away. I turned toward my bedside clock and saw that it was 10:00 a.m. I knew, in the dialysis unit at Children's, Beau was beginning his second hour hooked up to the blood filtering machine.

My mind spent huge portions of each day focused on Beau's health. Had he thrown up more times than usual this week? What time this week were we scheduled to meet with the nephrology team? Had Beau received his most recent shipment of protein shakes in the dorm? Did he like French vanilla? Maybe he'd like to try a new flavor. Did the small dorm sized refrigerator keep the shakes cold? When Beau woke up did his ankles look swollen, or did they look normal? Was Beau remembering not to salt his chicken breast at lunch? Was his face pale?

"Enough!" I threw the covers off and sat up in a single motion. My sweet puppies, who had been cuddled next to me, jumped to the floor and shook themselves awake. "Yes, Beau is sick." I acknowledged the idea and rubbed my hand from the top of my forehead down to my chin, clearing my thoughts. "But I am well!" I even closed my eyes and envisioned the words:

| I am well.

On this unremarkable Wednesday, I discovered that my obsessive thinking about my child's illness would have to find a point of separation. I stood up and wiggled my bare toes into the thick carpet on the floor. I took two or three big deep breaths. My lungs were clear. I felt my own heartbeat gently pitter patter against the walls of my chest. I rubbed my hand along my collarbone. No dialysis port for me. I could have a chicken breast for lunch – pour an entire shaker of salt all over it – chew it up, choke it down, and my kidneys would be just fine!

"Casey!" I said with empowerment, "It is okay that you aren't sick!" I threw my teal comforter back over the pillows.

"Why," I wondered, "doesn't Greg worry about Beau in the same continual way that I worry about Beau?" Greg loved Beau as fiercely as I loved him. There was no question about that. But as much as I felt responsible for Beau being sick, Greg felt responsible for Beau being a survivor.

I threw on my running shoes, attached the dogs to their leashes, and headed outside. While I ran the familiar dusty road and watched the forest squirrels scampering from tree to tree, I wondered how I would begin to compartmentalize Beau's sickness, as Greg had done.

"Has Beau had more well days in his life than sick days?" I thought. "Absolutely. Yes."

Why not, during the times when a lab result wasn't quite what we hoped for, or Beau had a day of throwing up that was particularly rough, start spending some time thinking about all the times Beau's days have not been rough – or all of the times Beau threw-up before baseball but went on to play the game. Beau had a pretty good record at survival so far. One hundred percent!

I needed to spend some of my thinking time focused on Beau's strengths. I needed to let those reminders of Beau overcoming sepsis and enduring physical therapy spend their time sitting at the forefront of my brain. Also, I needed to let go of the factors surrounding Beau's diagnosis that I could not control. I could not affect Beau's creatinine. Turning to prayer seemed to be a welcome resolution.

When I felt particularly defeated by Beau's sickness, I had indeed texted the words, "God probably doesn't exist anyway," but my background told me otherwise. Before my parents were married, my Daddy spent two years in seminary training to become a priest. A priest! He loved the ceremonial side of Catholicism. When we attended mass during my childhood, Daddy appreciated the routine of kneeling and standing. If it was a calendar Sunday that required the burning of incense, I looked forward to watching him close his eyes and inhale giant gulps of our priest's holy smoke. For all the love my parents showed practicing Catholicism, I had a skeptical answer. I didn't believe God was fake. I always felt like

was something bigger, but I just couldn't get behind the
............ity of Catholicism.

In college, I started asking my Great Grandma Johnson to
tell me about how she talked with God. I remember I specifically asked how she talked with *her* God, and she smiled. Rhoda
Johnson had lived to be 99 years old. She died when Beau was
two. I felt a kinship with her that guided me through most of my
twenties, and when it came to faith and prayer, it seemed like she
had a direct line to God.

Long before I was born, Grandma Rhoda grew tired of the
hell fire and brimstone style of church in which she was raised.
"I've never thought God was scary," she told me , more than once.
"I don't think we're put on this earth to fear God." Grandma Rhoda
thought God was all about love. She also didn't think human
judgment should make its way into the brick-and-mortar walls
of any church. With those ideas in mind, when she was roughly
forty just around World War II, Grandma Rhoda started her very
own country church in the community building on the prairie
of Peyton, Colorado. She named her church: The Open Door. I
loved knowing that. Within The Open Door, people prayed freely,
sang loudly, and praised God without fear of judgment. My Great
Grandma was not the pastor. She far preferred to play the organ.
Instead, she found a young minister with a deep understanding
of The New Testament, and he led the flock where she and her
neighbors broke away from formal faith. My favorite prayer that
she ever shared with me said: *Thank You, God. I am strong, I am
healthy, and I am able. Amen.*

I slowed my jog to a walk, and repeated Grandma's prayer.

"Pups," I said, "I'm gonna replace the I in Grandma's prayer
with *Beau.*"

Thank You, God. Beau is strong, Beau is healthy, and Beau is able. Amen.

The dogs just wagged, but I felt a hint of power over my worry. Was this single prayer going to change everything? Absolutely not. But it felt so freeing to hand some of the weight of Beau's sickness over to a power that was bigger than all of us. I was also cautious and a little bit sorry. I had blamed God for not saving Beau from kidney failure. I still sort of thought God wasn't showing up in the way I thought he should. But, if I was fair, I also knew that God had filled more of my life with miracles than sorrow.

By the end of my run, I had a plan. I would focus on all the times Beau's strength of character and endurance had served him. I would use Grandma Rhoda's prayer, and I would set aside a compartment in my mind for worrying. Worrying would not take over my days.

Finally, I would be glad about the fact that I was well, and I would remind my brain of my own wellness as often as I remembered.

— 21 —
A New Way Forward

Beau's kidneys were declared "completely failed" in October. The declaration was somewhat ceremonious. One of Beau's doctors presented us with a formal document while Beau sat in the dialysis chair, and I sat beside him. Between February of his freshman year in college and the early fall of his sophomore year as a biology major, Beau's acute diagnosis became permanent. The word "acute" had been thrown around his medical diagnosis often because kidney failure had hit Beau so hard and so quickly. Until October, the nephrology team had kept some hope that remission would occur. In fact, the original catheter placed in Beau's chest was envisioned as temporary; the hope was that dialysis for Beau would last a week or two until his kidney function improved. The team's hope gave me hope. Originally, when friends asked us if Beau would eventually need a transplant, I generically answered that I didn't think so. But it turned out, none of us was particularly realistic.

At each stage of trying to stop Beau's kidney failure, his kidneys worked a little less. None of the protocol worked. Dialysis sessions that began as two-hour-long sessions in July became three-and-half-hours-long in October. Why? Beau's kidneys stopped performing any filtration. His body almost completely stopped making pee. If I spent all day with him or we had a long lunch and some extra time to sit talking, Beau never needed to use the restroom. That fall, the nephrology team re-stated Beau's acute diagnosis as complete kidney failure. Scientifically, they estimated Beau's kidney function at just under 7 percent.

"You ready to sign this puppy?" The doctor asked. She handed Beau the pen and formal document.

"Ready for a new plan." Beau stated. He signed away his native kidneys with a flourish.

Beau smiled the big smile. We shared a weird lightness in the failure. Failed. At every turn. Each attack we mounted on Beau's Lupus nephritis gave way to more problems, and we were finally forced to raise the white flag. Beau fought bravely, and he was tired. So, the moment when my son gave up his native kidneys on paper, I was not sad. His signature meant we were stepping back, refueling, and preparing for a different battle. While this may have seemed like yet another chance for me to cry in public, I didn't feel sorrowful. This time, I felt hopeful.

I felt like we were signing a truce with Beau's body – the acceptance that we weren't going to fight with this broken equipment any longer – and it brought immense relief. There would be no more forced protocol. No more chemo. No additional kidney biopsies with his native kidneys. Beau and his doctor agreed on an official paper document that his kidneys were used up. Once that happened, the plan of treatment took a dramatic turn and we felt renewed faith. Beau and his doctors would immediately begin the work of making him healthy enough to receive a kidney transplant.

Transplant Evaluation

The very next week, we met with the transplant team at Children's Hospital. Things began to move quickly. While the nephrology department declared Beau's kidneys completely failed, more people in more departments had to get on board with the plan for a transplant. Being cleared for a transplant involves a multi-day transplant evaluation that considers such varying criteria as a patient's vaccine records, their dental health, heart health, mental stability and overall chance at surviving after major surgery.

Dr. Marsh would have to agree that Beau's Lupus was in check. Before she would sign off on a transplant, Beau would have to exist more than five months without a Lupus flare-up. This meant that he would continue to receive weekly blood draws. We always strove for Beau to be flare-up free, but now the stakes were higher. A flare-up would reset the clock on an impending transplant. Beau longed for the fresh start and energy of a new kidney.

"But f–," I said.

On this new journey toward a transplant, Beau willed, I prayed, and Greg would muscle them away. Beau did the math and determined that as long as he remained flare-up free, the soonest he could be considered for a transplant was March of 2020.

"If Beau had gone into kidney failure when he was seventeen, or any time before he officially became an adult, he might have been on a kidney waiting list behind just one or two kids."

Our transplant nurse, Kim, explained. "Now that Beau is an adult, he is in a line behind hundreds of people waiting for a new kidney."

Colorado, Utah, and Wyoming were each in our region. In the kidney world, adults of every age wait on the same transplant list for their lives to be made whole again. It seemed gruesome to ask Kim where most kidney donations came from, but I simply didn't know. Was there a certain age when a kidney became too old? Too old to be viable for donation? Also, since humans have two kidneys, was a kidney donation *really* only one organ?

I threw each of these garbled questions out at once, and Kim ably answered.

"Here's the good thing about kidneys," she began, "they do not have to be harvested from a deceased donor. A living donor who matches Beau's blood type as well as some additional antibody tests, can donate to him. Most people can live just fine with one kidney.

When Beau is declared ready for transplant, he will receive one kidney."

Kim also explained that a kidney is considered viable for donation up to age 55.

Neither Greg nor I was 50 yet. That was good. We also heard the hard news that many kidney donations *do* come from deceased donors and with a regional waiting list of more than five hundred people, Beau would likely wait five to seven years for a deceased donor's kidney. She said that some very healthy organ donations came from drug overdoses. This final stat and the reality that my child could spend years on dialysis, was heavy.

Kim had given me a spiral notepad at the start of our day, and I wrote in big letters: "NEED LIVING DONOR."

We sat in a comfortable board room while representatives from various departments within the hospital revolved in and out, asking interview questions that ranged from "How often does Beau pee?" to "What level of anxiety does the hospital atmosphere create for your family??" For me, I was actually least worried about Beau when we were in a controlled environment. His life as a college student living on a downtown campus was not controlled, so I worried. I worried while I also wanted him there. I hoped, with fingers crossed, that he was playing intramurals and going out for Thai food. There was a restaurant within walking distance from campus called Swing Thai, and when Beau was feeling well, he liked anything on their menu. Greg and I agreed that Beau belonged at college, in person, because it gave him a spark.

On the occasions when Beau had been hospitalized, there was certainly some peace for me in sleeping on a plastic couch five feet across the room. Together, in the hospital, I worried less. This was one of the questions I fielded from the transplant team. Were hospital visits filled with complete anxiety for me? No. Hospital visits were pit stops away from reality. I liked having an eye on my kid, but Beau needed to be out in the world. I explained that as a mom, the hospital atmosphere felt peaceful. I wondered if that answer gave me a thumbs-up on the transplant team's survey.

We wanted thumbs-ups by the handful. It would be great to look good both on paper and in person. One of the biggest positives for Beau, in the consideration of the transplant team, was his perfect attendance as a dialysis patient. Even as a full-time student, he managed to never miss one single dialysis treatment.

A hospital psychiatrist was among the many visitors to our room that day. It wasn't just Beau who was being thoughtfully considered. Transplant recipients receive the actual gift of life, and it comes with new terms. The psychiatrist who spoke with us wanted to be clear: Beau would be taking anti-rejection medicines for his entire life. Twice a day. Every day. Was he competent to do it? Was our family strong, worthy, and stable enough for the bumps ahead? This interviewing process reminded me of becoming adoptive parents.

Ten years earlier, when we knew our family was not complete, Greg and I opened our lives and our world up to adoption. We were interviewed over several days by our adoption caseworker, Julia, whose task it was to determine that our family was strong, worthy, and stable enough for the bumps ahead. At the time of our adoption vetting, I was 39 and Greg was 40. Julia emphasized, during at least three pre-adoption interviews, that because we were *older* parents, a birth Mom was less likely to choose us. I preferred the term "experienced parents," to the term *old*. We brushed the warning away and presented our best selves. Middle age had given us both the contentment and patience that were far less tangible in our twenties.

"I'll be more eager than ever to push a swing and ride bikes." I remember saying.

Greg, Bailey, Beau, and I received the supernatural gift of baby Beck just six weeks after completing all the adoption formalities. Beck's birth mom was our hero.

"Lucy" was a junior in high school when she dropped out of classes because her growing pregnant belly was making it hard for other kids in school to concentrate.

Greg and I met Lucy when she had just seven weeks left in a very unplanned pregnancy. Lucy had no dad – at least not a dad she knew – and her first question was for Greg.

"You love babies, don't you?" She spoke bravely and smiled.

"I love them." Greg replied. He set his big hands on the table cupped over the top of mine.

I jumped in, "He's a baby whisperer. Both of our big kids did their best napping on their Daddy's chest."

Lucy said she thought so. In the pictures we had shared of our little family, before Lucy asked to meet us, she noticed that Greg was very cuddly.

"You both look so fun." She added. "I chose you because I want this little boy to have a fun life. I want him to have a stable life."

I told Lucy how thankful I was for her time with us; that I had been born to a mother who was seventeen when I arrived, and that she, too, loved me above everything else.

The following week, Lucy invited me to her ultrasound appointment where I saw the first live pictures of our new son. She and I both giggled and held each other's hand as he tumbled around. It seemed he was trying to avoid the technician's wand.

Middle age did not hinder our ability to adopt in any way. I took the message in this gift to be: Never presume hurdles in front of your goal. There is no purpose served by taking time to create imaginary challenges. –We discovered in adoption, as we would in the pursuit of a kidney for Beau, that some hurdles are real, and others are imagined. Additionally, we learned not to be swayed by assumption. We believed in going for it. We were gung-ho!

The long day of kidney interviews lasted until just before dark. Kim said she knew Beau was already planning for a March transplant. She warned him not to get his hopes up. I explained, "We've been here before. We experienced a miracle adopting Beau's younger brother. Maybe there's another miracle out there for us."

Kim smiled, "I hope there is."

We all shook hands and agreed that within the following

week, Beau and I would meet with a urologist and a cardiologist. We needed confirmation on two more aspects of Beau's overall health: Would his bladder be able to withstand a new kidney? Could his heart endure the surgery? The following week, both answers came back as a resounding, Yes!"

— 23 —
There's Always a Chance
(or) Never Say Never

People over the age of forty commonly stop saying things like: "No way, not possible, can't happen." Our daughter Bailey says these things often. In her twenties, there is very little gray. She is exactly one quarter of a century younger than me, and my experiences have proven time and time again that almost everything is possible – at least once. Bailey has not made the same discovery yet.

For example, it can rain during complete sunshine. I have seen it happen in Colorado and Hawaii – a startling phenomenon! On another front, watermelons can be yellow. Carrots can be purple. Dogs can like cats, and in the hunt for a living kidney donor for Beau, I had to stick to the lessons life had shown me. I had to believe it would happen. I also did not believe the donor could be Greg, but I did not say it was impossible.

Once Beau was approved by the transplant team, which happened in late October, we were not permitted to immediately start testing potential donors. While Beau was under the care of Children's hospital, a potential donor would be under the care of the hospital next door, which was part of the University of

Colorado hospital system. Beau's donor would have an entirely separate transplant team.

This second transplant team was completely devoted to the long-term health of the donor. For their purposes, Beau was secondary, and the donor was paramount.

I thought of the two organ donation teams as professional sports agents. Each group of agents advocated for their "client." Team Donor would not okay an individual to donate his or her kidney if it meant jeopardizing the donor's long-term health. Team Recipient would not okay Beau for transplant until his health was entirely stable, and the donated kidney was an excellent match. The process of vetting a potential kidney donor is so involved that the folks who do go on to become living donors are among the very healthiest members of society.

Donor blood type

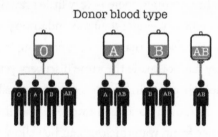

Recipient blood type

Here are some of the factors the transplant team at University hospital considered as they sought a donor for Beau that included blood type, diabetes risk, use of medications, and much more. Potential donors could apply online. Beau was three months flare-up free when this search began. All forty pounds of the excess water weight he had been carrying since going into kidney failure was gone. Dialysis had done its job.

He seemed on track for a miraculous spring transplant. I wrote on Facebook something like, "Let the kidney search begin!"

Up until December, Beau had made me promise to keep his battle with kidney failure off social media. Once University Hospital gave the okay for us to begin searching for a healthy donor, Beau said I could pull out all the stops. He didn't really say *all the stops*; he said I could mention his need for a kidney on Facebook. Once. So, I mentioned the need, once. The responses humbled me. They humbled our entire family. One acquaintance from Beck's first grade class, a wonderful mom with whom I planned a fundraiser, was the first to reach out via text.

"I lost a very dear friend in college." She wrote. "He was the first person I ever knew who donated their organs." She typed that her dear friend lived on in the many lives his organs saved. She still really missed him. She also explained that, as a mother, she couldn't imagine my worry.

"How do you sleep?" she asked.

She filled out the online questionnaire, made it through the first stage of questions, and participated with her whole heart in the second stage of testing which involved a 24-hour urine catch. Every time she peed, over a 24-hour t period, she collected it. The most amazing part of this woman offering one of her kidneys to Beau was the reality that she had never even met him! Following her second stage of testing, our first potential donor was knocked out of the running. It was evident from her urine samples that she had kidney stones. Still, this acquaintance had given us so much hope in the overwhelming goodness of most human beings.

While we received word via text and email that one or two additional friends were being tested as potential donors, Greg, Bailey, and I also began the process. At age 22, Bailey endured her first ever blood draw simply to see if she was a blood type match for her brother. Yes! A+. Each of us were compatible blood types for Beau. With this news, I expected the search for Beau's kidney to be easy.

— 24 —
Not Fitting the Mold

As a high school wrestler, Greg stood out from the crowd. He didn't just stand out in high school. Greg was also excellent in the *world* of collegiate wrestlers and was able to travel throughout Europe as a Junior Olympian. All of this happened years before we met in college. Even BC (before Casey) Greg was an athletic superstar. By the time we were twenty, Greg's biceps and shoulders stretched the seams of every double extra-large shirt he owned. He was massive.

When we first began dating, I loved that Greg would pick me up in his arms and lift me into the passenger seat of his Ford Bronco. He was somewhat of a born athlete and somewhat of a competitive freak. He did not like to lose, or even say the word "lose" out loud. Being a big guy helped with the winning. From the very day Greg turned twelve, his body mass index (BMI) was off the proverbial charts, and it had always benefited him in life. Plot twist: A big body mass is a negative on the chart of donor viability. As a potential kidney donor, clearing the BMI target weight for someone his size created Greg's first hurdle. Listening in on his initial phone conversation with the kidney donation coordinator from University Hospital, I could not help but laugh. The nurse on the other end of the line was questioning Greg's weight compared with his modest height of 5'11."

"I am sort of a muscular guy," Greg explained apologetically. "I have done some weightlifting, and I work construction every day."

Wait, what? *Some weightlifting?* Let me be clear. Greg's love of the gym didn't fade with his Olympic aspirations, and Greg turned a large portion of our basement into a carnival of free weights before Beau was out of diapers. Lifting is Greg's second favorite activity, behind coaching baseball. However, it was clear that the donation coordinator, nurse Sally, had heard this type of explanation for a heavier BMI before.

"When I see you, if you're cut like a swimwear model, we can reconsider the BMI recommendation." Sally replied. I thought she was a little too salty, having never met him. Greg liked her spunk. Ultimately, after that first call, she did not immediately disqualify Greg as a donor for simply being too heavy on paper. She scheduled an appointment for us to meet in person and planned a CT scan so that Greg's kidneys could be viewed for overall health. Once Greg hung up the phone, he said he would take that one as a win.

Several days later, Greg and I visited University hospital for his initial exam and introduction to Team Recipient. Sally, along with the head nephrologist and a nurse practitioner, circled around Greg, who was seated at a small table, and talked about him like he wasn't there.

"He is a muscular guy." The nephrologist reasoned.

"Yeah. Look at his biceps." Sally agreed. In that instant, it wouldn't have surprised me for her to purr like a cougar, except that Sally really was extremely professional, and I was one hundred percent searching for *any* reason to find humor in the heavy quest for Greg to become Beau's donor. After the three medical professionals talked amongst themselves for several minutes longer, the nurse practitioner measured Greg's neck. She affixed stickers to his chest and ran an echocardiogram for several seconds. The test of his heart really was quick. It was over before Greg knew it had officially started.

"Greg, you're done with this part," the nurse practitioner advised.

"Your son would be lucky to get one of your kidneys." Her warm smile filled the room.

Sally thanked us extensively for our time and explained that she would call Greg after the weekend to go over results from his cardiogram and CT scan.

"I think our team agrees that your BMI is not going to hold you up from donating. Just don't gain another pound." She smiled broadly.

"I understand." Greg nodded.

My selfless husband had never looked so beloved. Once we got into the car, I cried. Greg patted my leg. "Step at a time," He said, "Step at a time."

Beau texted me within minutes to see how the preliminary testing had gone. I felt like my answer should be balanced between hopeful but not overtly encouraging.

"Daddy's good." I typed. "We will hear more results from his testing on Monday. How do you feel today?"

"Pretty good." Beau replied. I made a mental note that most mommas of nineteen-year-olds probably didn't end every communication with "How do you feel today?" But until Beau lived with a functioning kidney, I would wonder how he felt every moment of every day because I had an underlying fear that dialysis was just borrowed time.

— 25 —
Overcoming Donation Obstacles

It was never a surprise when I woke Greg up at one or two in the morning and asked him to switch sides. Tap. Tap. Tap. First, I'd knock on his shoulder and then push him a little bit if the tapping didn't work. He had a way of snoring that was almost rhythmic, except for the occasional gigantic snarl that rose from the depths of his throat and then stopped – along with his breathing. Mostly, I was used to this and to the long pauses between breaths that sometimes accompanied his snoring. However, every so often, Greg woke me up with the throaty clatter. Asking him to roll over usually fixed the problem.

Everyone in our home threw around the term sleep apnea.

If we shared a hotel room on a family vacation, Beau would always come to breakfast and say "I could hear Dad snoring the *entire* night. Bring it down a notch, big boy."

"Yep," Bailey would chime in, "everyone now, say it together, what does Dad have?"

Then we all would shout out together, "Dad has sleep apnea!"

I never considered snoring to be a true health concern. I quickly learned differently when Sally called Greg to discuss his cardio and lab results. He was shocked when it came to sharing what his tests revealed. "Casey, remember how the nurse last week recorded my heartbeat for all of three seconds?" Greg asked, sounding astonished. He didn't wait for my reply. "Anyway, they determined that I have sleep apnea, which can cause an irregular heartbeat."

"Seriously?" I wondered how in the world a three second echocardiogram revealed any details about Greg's heart. I flashed back to his mom, at 52, dead from a pulmonary embolism. My own heart was torn between devastation that Greg would likely not be considered as a donor for Beau and gratefulness that, with the discovery of an irregular heartbeat, my sweet husband would see many more birthdays than his late mother, our "Saint Frances."

"So . . . did she say you are a no for Beau?" I asked. I asked, but I knew.

Greg didn't immediately answer. "Also," he said, now shaking his head from side to side,

"I have a tapeworm. And since I am not immediately able to be Beau's donor, she said I could choose whether or not to get rid of it."

Why would anyone who knew they had a tapeworm choose to keep it? Would they name it? I hung my head in my hands. I debated which question to start with. Greg was on a bit of a rant.

"Obviously," he continued, "I will take the dose of antibiotic required to get rid of my tapeworm. Sally said that one is any easy fix."

"Where," I wondered, "does one pick up a tapeworm?"

"Outside of the country." Greg answered.

Two years earlier, we had taken a dream vacation to Costa Rica. We had gone swimming in deep, black fishing holes. All three Gent boys" had spent countless hours body surfing in the rugged ocean. Maybe Greg's tapeworm had been with us since that trip. As creepy as it sounded, the tapeworm was not Greg's biggest hurdle to becoming Beau's donor.

With sleep apnea, the irregular heartbeat and slightly high blood pressure that it caused, a tapeworm, and the reality that he had never had a colonoscopy, Greg would not be cleared by Team Donor.

I didn't know what to say. I was sad and mad. I couldn't explain the anger, because it was somewhat of a gift to learn that Greg had hidden health concerns. Beyond this glimmer of good, the number seven stood out in an ugly way at the forefront of my mind. Seven years would be the likely amount of time Beau would be tethered to dialysis without the discovery of a living donor.

Greg and I had been standing in the master bathroom. I walked over to our bed and punched my pillow. I punched and punched it.

"Why can't *one thing* go our way?" I asked Greg and the walls of my room and maybe God, who was listening.

"I am not *out*." Greg reiterated. "I am for sure delayed for three months, but Sally said the sooner I can see a sleep apnea specialist, the better. That is my next step."

I did the math. Three months would be April, *if* Greg's sleep apnea could be reasonably fixed, his blood pressure improved, and the tapeworm eliminated. Additionally, he would have to have a colonoscopy and get wonderful results. It felt like a tall order of "what ifs." Because what if three months rolled around and none of Greg's underlying problems were cured? Each of us knew that the search for Beau's living donor had to continue.

"Oh, there was one good thing," Greg blurted, "part of the testing involved mixing my blood with a sample of Beau's blood. And that was good. Really good. Sally said they expect one or two antigens to form against the donor's blood, but Beau's blood did not form a single antigen against mine."

I thought that sounded good, but I didn't think it mattered. We had to find another match.

— 26 —
Fun and the Unknown

"Mom, fire again!" Beau yelled. "It's the red button. Push it!"

"Push the button, Momma, the red one." Beck giggled.

We were jostling around the exceedingly small cockpit of the newest Star Wars ride in Disneyland. My hip slammed into the wall of the ride as we took an extraordinarily rough turn. I was assigned the detail of the gunner. Beck was our pilot. Greg, Beau, and Bailey were along for the reckless ride. I breathed it in with delight. Beau smiled bigger and wider than I had seen in months. The ride threw us from side to side. Beck's piloting appeared to fly us straight into a space sand dune and just as quickly as we had "taken off," our starship landed. Ride over.

"Mom," Beau wrapped his arm around my shoulders as we exited. "Next time, I will be the gunner."

I hugged him, and for a split second, Beau rested his chin on the top of my head.

"When did that happen?" I wondered aloud. "Have I shrunk?"

"Probably," Bailey chimed in. "You are *really* old."

It was dusk – my favorite time of the day in any Disney park – and the five of us walked between rides together, laughing. We had hoped to take a four-day vacation while Beau and Beck were on holiday break, but after I booked the trip, Beau's nephrology team said that he absolutely couldn't skip a day of his scheduled dialysis appointments. I had assumed (incorrectly) that missing a Monday of dialysis and returning for dialysis on Tuesday would be acceptable. Beau's main doctor said *no* to my plan.

"I can find a dialysis clinic in Anaheim for Beau to go to," she explained, "but his kidneys just aren't doing any filtering, and he cannot go Saturday, Sunday, and Monday with no treatment."

This was Beau's reality. He made an effort every single day of college to live a normal college life. I made a point of scheduling small getaways and fun activities for our family, but kidney failure set boundaries within which we were forced to function. Our January trip to Disneyland wound up being three days of magic rather than four. Beau was continuing to have no symptoms of a Lupus flare-up, and the dialysis team at Children's Hospital had been administering Beau's treatments remarkably well since July. We opted to avoid the unknown, and to reject a dialysis clinic in Anaheim. Our trip would have to be shortened.

Having one family member with a grave illness gave each of us renewed appreciation when it came to this visit to Disneyland. On the simplest level of gratefulness, Beck said he was glad he had two kidneys that worked. Our whole family nodded wildly in agreement. Bailey said she was thankful **not** to have to get blood drawn several times each week. Beau shrugged his shoulders, saying that part wasn't too bad.

It was our third and last day in the park, and Beau was enjoying his second cone of the delicious pineapple ice cream that is found tucked inside of a tiki hut, in Adventureland, just off Main Street USA.

Patients in kidney failure need to avoid certain foods that are high in phosphorus or potassium. It had been more than six months since Beau had enjoyed salsa, mashed potatoes, or fries. His legs looked like little spindles, and his jeans hung off of his waist. Losing the forty pounds of water weight through his rigorous devotion to dialysis did wonders for Beau's overall health, but as we entered 2020, my son looked extraordinarily frail. I watched him shape the sides of his pineapple dessert with a plastic spoon, and I felt profusely grateful that the three-day trip even happened.

During dinner on our final night, I told the family that when we got back to Colorado, I would begin being tested to be Beau's donor.

"I hope you can't," Beck whispered.

His candor stunned me for a second. I hadn't expected any push back, but Beck was eight. Beau's sickness had taken a toll on each of us. For the entire previous summer, Beck watched Beau lay on the couch cushions and sleep the days away. He listened from upstairs all the times that Beau threw up in the downstairs bathroom.

"Mom," Bailey chimed in, "I'm sure it worries Beck to think of you going to the hospital."

"I am not going to the hospital yet." I assured everyone. "Also, the doctors won't let me give Beau a kidney unless it's super safe."

"Hey," Greg teased, "I might still get to give Beau *my* kidney. A step at a time."

We all sat around the table in silence for a few minutes longer. Riders on Big Thunder Mountain Railroad screamed in contrast. On days like this one, it seemed like our little family lived in its own kidney universe with the rest of the world speeding by around us. We were doing the best we could – believing in no wasted days, but existing on a sort of pause button – until a kidney was found for Beau. He stood up from the table.

"Let's go ride the fastest train in the wilderness!" Beau's smile gleamed as he glanced around the table, making eye contact with each of us.

Everyone jumped up and headed to the next ride. I walked behind my three precious kids and grabbed Greg's hand in mine. Hundreds of bodies moved in and out around us. Families like ours, no doubt many in their own health battles, were enjoying Disneyland. Other families who weaved around us may have had no health issues at all. And while I deeply believed no person is ever singled out to be sick, I also strengthened my resolve that it was okay to be mad. God didn't choose for Beau to have failed kidneys. I did not believe God wanted my child or anyone else's child to get sick and walking through the happiest place on earth I gave myself permission to have some difficult, bitter moments. Disneyland wasn't the time for it, but I realized that pain is relative.

While your family may have been hurt harder or deeper than mine, your family's great struggle doesn't minimize my family's pain from a comparative scratch. The opposite is also true. Pain is pain. Sick is sick. Sad is sad. I caught myself glancing at a child in a wheelchair, and my first reaction was: "At least Beau can still walk." Nope. I decided, in the line at Jungle Cruise, to stop comparing. I didn't want to be someone who thought about how much worse Beau had it than someone else or how much better off we were than the next person.

I am not the first Momma to experience grief. I am hardly the first to watch her child struggle. In our pain and in our struggle, we are the same. We are the warriors who care and caretake. None better. None worse. None more or less deserving than the next. This was profoundly humbling.

I also strengthened my resolve that nothing is deserved. We each earn some of the good that comes our way, we may reap some

of the bad, but it is clear inside of my own heart and thou
that deservedness plays **no** part in our free will, hard work, faith,
immunity, grave diagnosis, resilience, or dumb luck. As Greg so
often says, "Everybody is just trying to do their best."

— 27 —
Setbacks

Sometime in February, I announced on Facebook, with an abundantly heavy heart, that I could not be Beau's donor. I hadn't made it as far along in the testing process as Greg. I met the weight requirement, though Sally did ask me how I would feel about losing seven pounds. I said I could try, but that I already jogged every day and kept up with my eight-year-old. She laughed. I had the correct blood type, so I participated in the 24-hour urine test where I was required to collect my pee every time I visited the restroom. The process made me feel nervous and like I needed to pee constantly. Greg picked up pizzas for dinner so I wouldn't have to gather my urine in a public restroom.

The next morning following my urine collection, I sat in the lab area of the hospital for several hours while they tested my blood for diabetes. I had three blood draws that morning: one upon my arrival, the second after I drank a high-content glucose mix, and the third test two hours after I ingested the glucose cocktail. The entire time, I sat reading a five-year-old *Good Housekeeping* magazine from 2014, texting with my Momma, and wondering how in the world Beau sat at dialysis for four hours three times a week. I could barely survive my one morning of labs!

Beau amazed me. I did not text him to say that I was bored out of my ever-loving mind. When I left the lab, my technician said I passed the glucose tests within standard.

Sally called me Tuesday morning.

"Are you having your period?" She asked.

"No." I replied.

"Hmmm. I wish the answer were 'Yes.'" She said. She explained that I had too high of a protein count in my urine to be a donor. She thought that if I were having my period, that might account for blood in the urine, which would have made my protein count high. No luck.

"Can I do another urine collection?" I practically begged. "Maybe I didn't get clean catches." My mind was spinning. I sat down at the kitchen table. Would I really be turned away this early in the process?

"You can't be tested again for six months." Sally spoke quickly before I could interrupt. "I am sorry Casey, but there are other people being tested for Beau. I am working to find a donor for your son every day."

"I know you are." I said, reminding my heart to be grateful. "Thank you, Sally."

I clicked my phone off. Just like that, my day fell over. I walked back to the bedroom and flopped sideways into bed. Who else did we know who might be trying to donate their kidney to Beau? HIPAA rules protected the information of potential donors, so Sally couldn't give me any names. She had simply said, "*There are other people,*" which led me to assume there were at least two anonymous folks going through the same steps I had just failed. However, while my urine did contain some protein, I did not have diabetes. On to the next candidate...I decided to text Beau the good news before the bad.

"Do you know if any of your friends are trying to be your donor?" I asked.

"Landon tried." Beau answered. "But he has an autoimmune disease, too. Remember? They rejected him."

"Hmmm. That guy Landon is a good friend." I replied. "Sally says other people are testing."

"Mom, what about you?"

"Buddy," long pause, "I am a no. There's protein in my urine."

"What do you do about that?" Beau wondered aloud.

I explained that Sally told me I could follow up with my primary care doctor. I didn't plan on it.

"Well..." Beau's typing lingered off. "I'm not getting my hopes up."

"How do you feel?" I asked. No answer. I could imagine how he felt: Rundown. Overwhelmed. Disappointed. I felt it too.

"Daddy's doing well on the CPAP," I inserted.

Immediately following our trip to Disneyland, Greg had gotten an appointment to see a sleep specialist. Evidently, this doctor reminded Greg of Brian Wilson, a chill, hippy beach guy out of the sixties, who somehow ended up in Colorado. "Brian Wilson" prescribed a CPAP machine to improve Greg's breathing while he slept. I was amazed that my husband could literally fall asleep donning a SCUBA-type mask attached to plastic tubing, but Greg's snoring abruptly stopped, cold turkey.

Beau didn't text anything further. I had noticed this pattern in our communication; when the heaviness of finding a donor began to set in, Beau moved on to something else. Or he simply turned off his phone to preserve his sanity.

More than 199 people "liked" my Facebook post where I begged anyone who might want to be a living kidney donor to contact our university hospital. Since I spent most of my time immersed in the culture of kidney stuff, I studied my list of Facebook likes over and over. Who, I puzzled, was trying to be Beau's donor?

Meanwhile, the same week that I mourned being taken out of the running, I drove Greg to his required colonoscopy. He had a calm tenacity about slowly ticking off the requirements laid out for him to be reconsidered. If my math was correct, at best, Greg might be reevaluated in mid-April, three months following his visit with the sleep apnea specialist. A big part of me thought Greg was wasting his time. A smaller, louder part of me scolded myself for having any doubt. How dare I? Greg had already made it further in the testing process than I had. Reluctantly, I drove Greg to his procedure.

"You are the youngest guy we've seen in here for a year!" One of the nurses commented.

"Yep. Not yet fifty." Greg replied. He wore a hospital gown and a surgical cap. He wasn't up for small talk. Thankfully, the doctor who entered gave Greg's nurse a sufficient explanation for why she was prepping a patient who couldn't yet collect Social Security.

"This guy is my hero." The doctor explained. "He's here today to get one step closer to donating a kidney to his son."

One hour later, we were celebrating Greg's successful colonoscopy over pancakes, bacon, and more bacon. Greg gave a lovely toast while holding up his coffee cup.

"I don't have to go back for ten years, baby!" He beamed. He had zero polyps. Polyps would have been another reason that Greg could have been excluded as a donor. He had none.

Another box was now checked on his quest to be reconsidered as Beau's donor. I felt proud.

— 28 —
Life Before Kidney Failure

For several nights in a row, during a biting cold week in early March, I lay awake thinking of Juneau, Alaska. During the long light days of summer, the trees on this water-soaked peninsula literally stretch out to touch the sky. Everywhere, everything is green.

Moss clings heavily to the forest trees and even to garden gates and retaining walls. I remembered that much to my surprise, Juneau is a temperate rainforest, and hiking boot footprints are quickly swallowed up by mud and water on practically every trail. The green, the water, the ocean, and the wild are more vivid together than any combination of paints on a color wheel. The last time I truly remembered Beau robustly healthy was in Juneau.

The summer that he graduated from high school, Bailey took her dream job working with native Alaskans, who needed assistance finding food and housing, especially with children. For three weeks, she borrowed the car of a generous benefactor in Juneau and traveled from church to church sleeping on cots, reading to various toddlers, polishing several nails (for the first time ever), and helping their parents fill out employment and apartment applications. This was the very type of social healing work for which Bailey was built.

"And," she explained in an excited phone call several days before taking the job,

"You have always wanted to go to Alaska. Right? Momma, you have got to come visit!"

She left me no time to respond. Beau was sitting across the table from me in the kitchen.

"I have enough money to buy my own ticket." He smiled.

"Bailey, I'll come with her!!" Beau yelled across the table. He leaned forward on his elbows and said again, loudly, "Bailey, I will bring Mom!"

"Yeah!" She cheered on the other end. "I can't wait!"

The four of us were going to Alaska.

Back in the chilly sheets of my own bed as my mind fought sleep, I remembered how Beau and I ran nearly half a mile through the Seattle airport, almost missing our connection from Denver to Juneau. It hadn't phased Beau then, but I wondered how he would ever manage such a feat while suffering kidney failure. This was my consistent worry as the mother of Beau: Would his energy ever look the way it had *before*? Would Beau's life after kidney failure have any resemblance to life before kidney failure? The life he lived during kidney failure was a struggle, but I looked at it as the holding pattern before he landed – with a new kidney – into the life he would know as an adult.

I hoped for the return of the energetic Beau and wondered if every person who loved a gravely ill friend or family member shared the same fear. Was *I* more concerned about *my* reaction to Beau's becoming than he was? Probably. We expected to find a new normal upon transplant.

It was 3 a.m. As Greg slept soundly next to me, I held my cell phone in my hand and scrolled through photos from Alaska. We had hiked to Mendenhall Glacier. The glacial ice was a mixture of turquoise with intermittent threads of grey. It was a color I had never seen before, and it was magnificent. Beau was a specimen of health in these photos. His cheeks were pink, and his eyes sparkled.

On one of our daily drives along Juneau's winding roadways, we had pulled off the highway so Beau and Bailey could run through a meadow of animated blooms. Tall white feathery poofs stretched above the grass like nothing we'd ever seen in real life. I closed my eyes and smiled, before continuing to look more closely at the pictures of me from that dreamy time together. Without a doubt, I, too, was changed. In the past seven months, worry had aged me. Life between lab work, with so many unknowns, had furrowed a deeper wrinkle into my brow, and although I would never tell Bailey, within the past week, I had found three grey hairs!

Scrolling through the memories, I reconciled with our current situation of being smack in the middle of the "during" portion of Beau's journey. In our previous life, life before kidney failure, our biggest worry during our trip to Juneau was where to go for dinner. In the during portion of Beau's illness, the worry was greater. The stakes were higher. I understood that in the midst of it, in the grit of dialysis, we had to do more than just endure. Our lives had to count.

I eventually fell asleep, comforted by thoughts of the many ways Beau fit quality life into his current days.

Amazingly, even with dialysis, Beau continued as a full-time biology student. He made a spring trip to Rocky Mountain National Park with Greg, Beck, and I, where none of us could keep up with his snowshoeing speed. Beau led the family along frozen Bear Lake like a pro tour guide. Additionally, Beau collected unused bus passes from ten of his friends and classmates at Regis. There was a family he knew from dialysis who relied on the city bus to get to Children's Hospital, and Beau had been able to collect almost 30 bus passes for the family's use. Without question, even in sickness, Beau's life mattered.

The following morning, Greg woke me early. It was still dark behind the blinds above the bed.

"Casey," he shook my shoulder, "Sally just emailed. My sleep apnea doctor sent her a report from my sleep apnea machine. The transplant team liked the report! Sally said everything is for me to be the donor! I just need one more echocardiogram and for a cardiologist to sign off on it."

I was awake immediately. I went from lying flat to standing straight up next to the bed in an immeasurable blur. Step at a time. Step at a time. Greg had been meticulous about sleeping wearing his CPAP mask. More than eight weeks had passed, and the results his machine automatically generated must have looked incredibly positive. I grabbed Greg's scruffy face and kissed his forehead.

"Did Sally tell you which cardiologist to see?" I asked.

"I have a list of options." Greg answered. "I'll start calling their offices at 8 a.m."

He raced out of the bedroom. Then he came back.

"It's 5:59." Greg reported. After another minute or two, Beck stumbled through the doorway.

"Momma, what's going on?" he asked.

"Come give me hugs." I replied. I reached my arms all the way around his warm, sleepy body. "Daddy is another step closer to giving Beau his kidney."

— 29 —
How Is a Transplant Elective?

In the middle of a beautiful, sunny April afternoon, Beck and I lay in my big, rumpled bed talking about how sad we were. His head was propped against my shoulder, and his feet rested against a pillow, threatening to fall off the mattress. Along with the rest of the world, we were living in lockdown. Communities across the globe battled COVID-19. The overwhelming despair of the moment was not lost on my eight-year-old. For most of us, aged eight to ninety-eight, life was daunting. On this day, even the sunshine hadn't coaxed us out of bed.

"I'm sad too." I explained. I brushed my fingers lightly back and forth over Beck's skin. "I miss going to restaurants. I REALLY miss going with you to the park."

Beck said, "I miss seeing my friends in real life."

Beck's teacher was great about connecting the class online for lunchtime chats, and they had even attempted a virtual game of hot potato. Still, having no recess to play with his friends for more than a month felt depressing. There was no baseball practice, no playdates. For our family, the most depressing reality of living within the pandemic was that Beau had just turned twenty, and the chance for an impending transplant had disappeared. Colorado's governor, Jared Polis, declared that all transplants must be placed on hold.

"How in the world is a transplant considered elective?" I asked Greg. "There are people in need of hearts and lungs and livers. And Beau should have a new kidney by now."

"Transplants are elective for the person donating," Greg said. "Beau's transplant is not elective for Beau, but it is elective for me."

Greg's cardiology appointment several weeks earlier could not have gone better. In what could be considered a bright side to COVID, many cardiology offices had canceled any appointments that were not completely necessary. Because of the cancellations, Greg immediately got an appointment with one of the doctors Sally recommended. Upon reviewing a new echocardiogram, the doctor had said he would be honored to recommend Greg as a kidney donor. The recommendation was fabulous news. Other pandemic regulations were not so good.

While Beck and I delayed getting out of bed, Greg went on to say that Sally had even been ordered to stop scheduling organ donations from deceased donors. Those brave souls, with their spirits gone, still required ventilators to keep their organs viable. I hadn't thought of that! Coronavirus was wreaking havoc in every facet of healthcare, and it deeply impacted the community of survivors who were indefinitely on hold as they waited for life-saving organs.

I immediately wrote Governor Polis two letters, each begging him to lift his 30-day ban on organ transplants. From my Momma's heart perspective, the life of someone waiting for an organ should not be set aside for the life of a *potential* coronavirus patient. The very reality that there was NO ventilator shortage in Colorado weighed heavily on my logic. There were a lot of what-ifs, but what-ifs are just part of the daily journey for any person waiting on a life-saving organ. In Beau's case, every time his port was accessed and tied into the dialysis machine – every single Monday, Wednesday, and Friday morning – he risked infection. Beau's port was an open plastic tube that led straight from the outside world to his heart. I asked the governor not to trade one life for another.

This was a period when simply existing as the parent of a gravely ill child didn't make sense. I could not draw on the experiences of the moms and dads before me because there were none.

> No one had dealt with a transplant in the era of COVID. We were afloat in unchartered waters. A new sort of weight floated over me.

I was not particularly concerned about Beau catching COVID. He had very few chances to be exposed. Regis University, like almost every national college, had turned all their classes into virtual learning. Beau had moved back home a few weeks earlier, and each of his professors taught remotely. This was a hidden gift, I thought. If transplants were allowed to proceed within the next few months, Beau would be like every other college kid in America, but with one significant difference. Like the others, he would be learning at home. Unlike the others, Beau would also be recovering from transplant surgery! But that was the weight, and the heaviness, because we were not in charge. Children's Hospital was not in charge. Beau's surgeon was not in charge. COVID had taken over, and the government was mandating people's medical futures.

I felt like a fox in a cage. Of everyone in my immediate family, I was the most on edge about governmental policy dictating medicine. Both Beau and Greg went about their daily lives with purpose. I cannot count, nor would I like to, the number of times Greg repeated, "Step at a time."

This had been his mantra throughout the process to get approved as Beau's donor. It had served him well, but it made me crazy!

"Beau has done his part!" I would argue. "You have done your part! Let's do this!!"

"Would you like me to call Sally again?" He volunteered. "I will tell her 'You name a day, and we will be there.'"

"Yes." I smiled. "That would be great."

Greg called Sally again and explained that once the Governor's ban was lifted, he and Beau would literally be available at any given moment to proceed.

"How much notice will you need?" Sally inquired.

"One hour." He answered.

"Not realistic," she replied. "But, I like it."

— 30 —
Go Time

Greg's days on the job as a general contractor brought something new with every morning. He could be standing knee-deep in cement, helping pour a basement foundation, or he could be at the top of a 12-foot ladder preparing to place a sparkling new window in the vacant hole that waited.

Once, when Bailey was sixteen and babysitting Beck, she had tried to reach Greg by cell phone five times. I was shooting a wedding and made it my policy to leave my phone in the car. It turned out Bailey tried to stand up under an open glass window while filling Beck' baby pool, and her head took a sharp glass corner to the temple. Blood spurted all over the deck and into the pool. Unfortunately, it was "window day" at Greg's job site, and he wasn't answering his cell phone as he hung from the top of a ladder placing windows in the apex of a new home.

From everything that was relayed to me hours later, Bailey did not panic. Beck splashed around in a few inches of water while Bailey ran down a list of contacts in her cell phone. We, parents had failed miserably, but the first friend Bailey called picked up!

"I will come get you in 10," the friend replied.

Next, Bailey reached my daddy, who said he would be in charge of Beck.

I thought it all worked out fine! One friend held Bailey's hand as she screamed getting stitches, and my Daddy kept Beck away from the drama.

"Window Day," Bailey lamented, later. "I had to nick a precious artery NEAR MY BRAIN on Window Day!"

The doctor who stitched Bailey up had told her she just missed hitting an artery near her temple, and that if she had nicked the artery, they would be talking "buckets of blood." When Greg delivered Bailey the Starbucks drink, he picked up for her on his way home from the job site, she was sure to share the doctor's ominous words.

"I could still be laying on the deck, bleeding." She insisted. Making up for this one was going to take a few weeks. Bailey used all of her best tricks to make sure we both knew we had failed the emergency scenario.

"Why even have cell phones?" she prodded. "You guys might as well be living in the 1950s if you aren't going to use your phones, like when your only daughter needs you."

Yep, she was a "dram," which was Bailey's very own nickname for her own theatrical flair. It was never realistic to assume that Greg would answer his cell from the job site.

Again, on April 15, 2020, Greg did not pick up. This time, Sally, the transplant nurse and coordinator, called me directly.

"Mrs. Gent, can you get hold of Greg for me?" She skipped the formalities. "I just called and got his voicemail." No questions about Beau. She didn't ask how any of us were doing.

"Well, I'll sure try," I replied. In the back of my mind, I frantically considered whether or not I could travel all the back roads and drive myself to Greg's current job site. It wasn't as if he went to the same office every day. Besides, I had only visited this job site once. Asking Sally to share what was the urgency of her call would have been a waste of breath. I already knew she couldn't tell me anything because of HIPAA laws.

"If I can reach Greg," I fumbled, "he'll call you immediately."

My heart beat heavy and fast. Sally had not reached out to me since my failed attempt to become Beau's donor. I wondered what was going on. Quickly, I dialed each number to Greg's cell phone. I didn't dare try the speed button where his line was programmed into my phone; that could be quirky. I dialed. One, seven, one...it rang. His phone rang four times.

"Pick up!" I repeated, in a whisper. My fingers on the hand that wasn't holding my phone tapped nervously against my leg.

"Hello?" Greg answered. He sounded out of breath. But he picked up!

"Sally needs to get hold of you." I replied.

"What's going on?" He asked.

"I have no idea. Call me as soon as you know!" I hung up. Dang, I should have said,

"I love you." I also thought how glad I was that it wasn't window day.

While I waited to hear, Beck and I decided to go outside. I teased him that sitting in the house made the clock tick backward. Something we had been afforded, because of quarantine, was a lot of Momma and son outdoor time. Our bikes were parked in the driveway, just asking to be ridden, so we climbed on and started out down our path through the trees. We hadn't yet reached the road before my phone began vibrating madly against my front pocket.

"Hang on, Buddy," I called to Beck. "it's Daddy." Beck looped back through the pine trees and parked next to me.

"What's up?" I answered.

"April 21." Greg replied.

"What about April 21?" I wondered.

> ## "On April 21," Greg relayed solemnly, "I am giving Beau a new kidney."

"What?!"

"We have six days to wait!"

I screamed into the phone and the forest. Beck looked worried for an instant but saw that I was smiling. I was smiling in a way I hadn't thought I could smile. I laughed as I looked up to the blue Colorado sky with thanks.

"You tell Beau." I whispered into the phone.

"I'll call him now." Greg replied. "Is he in the house studying?"

"Nope. He's still at dialysis. Call him there." I suggested.

"Love you!" Greg said.

"I love you SO, SO much!" We hung up.

"Beck!" I grabbed his little, pudgy hands in mine and squeezed them.

"What's going on?" He smiled and pulled his hands back. They were soft and velvety, and I could hold onto them forever.

"Beau's getting his kidney!"

"He's getting Dad's kidney?" Beck implored.

"Yes. Daddy's kidney."

"Well, when Dad's done giving his kidney, I'll take care of Dad." He replied seriously.

"Daddy will like that." I answered.

We both got back on our bikes. I was shaking. I couldn't wait to hear what Beau said!

— 31 —
Pandemic Era Medicine

A number of things fit perfectly within six days. I realized, all at once, both how long it was and how short it was. Six days. Most of our trips to Hawaii lasted for six days. It was time enough to get a slight sunburn and watch it fade to tan, time enough to trek around a volcano, dance in the ocean, and eat too much island pineapple. Back on the mainland, most jugs of milk were good for about six days. Our family could last six days between trips to the grocery store, and six days was just the right amount of time to let pass between my longest six-mile runs.

Finally, that third week of April, both quickly and slowly, six days passed. It was transplant time!

Beau was cautiously optimistic. Would April 21st really be the first day of his best "new normal?" Was the transplant absolutely and officially approved by *everyone*? An infinite number of working parts, combining the staffs of two hospitals, would have to come together.

"We'll see, Dad." Beau had said. "There's a lot that can happen in six days."

Beau said we would celebrate, as a family, after it happened. He also said we would celebrate Dad. Greg was his hero.

The morning before April 21, I sat alone in my car, noticing the pastel array of paper face masks surrounding my seat. There were so many things I could have noticed or paid attention to on this momentous morning, but the masks represented a new way of life within the pandemic. I had developed a system. Masks I had worn once or twice were left on the console and were only to be reused in the case of a mask emergency.

According to a state mandate, masks were required to be worn at all times in public places. In light of COVID restrictions, our local King Soopers grocery store allowed just ten customers inside at one time. Casual lines formed at the store entrance. Everyone seemed to fear that the person six feet in front of, or six feet behind, him had coronavirus. Whole communities were told to "assume you have the virus." We were locked in fear.

In another even stranger pandemic-era encounter, just five minutes before I sat analyzing the masks inside my car, I had received a coveted COVID test. It was a requirement for Greg, Beau, and I to test negative for COVID in the last hours before transplant. I drove through a mobile COVID testing facility in the parking lot between University Hospital and Children's Hospital. I couldn't help but think that in under 24 hours, after so much physical effort from Greg and obedient daily preparation from Beau, a surgical technician would load Greg's kidney onto a golf cart, drive across the very same parking lot where I was being tested, and deliver Beau his new lease on life.

Once inside the testing garage, a nurse wearing light yellow paper scrubs, plastic gloves, a face mask, and a face shield, directed me to roll my window down. I leaned only my head out of the car window and squeezed my eyes tightly shut.

"It feels like the end of times," I texted.

I felt extremely isolated and couldn't imagine a more desolate time in America than this one. All the country, and most of the world, existed within the same uncertainty as I did, but I had an added glimmer of hope.

In the towering corridors behind me, Beau was already admitted as a patient. In the morning, he would become Denver's first COVID-era kidney transplant recipient. It was happening.

So, I sat. It would be at least four days until I could see Greg. The plan was for my Daddy to pick up Greg at 3 a.m. and deliver him to University Hospital. Beau and I would be sleeping somewhere inside the walls of Children's Hospital just next door. Greg would have to walk into the admitting area alone, in the weird blue darkness just before sun-up, and from that point forward, none of us could join him. The isolation of the process for Greg just felt like the heavy pull of gravity against my heart, and it sat lodged inside my throat like a stone. Greg was heroic. His selflessness was transcendent. Because of COVID, none of us would be holding his hand when he woke up from surgery. No Bailey. No Casey. Suddenly, there was this push-pull between celebrating Beau's transplant as a Momma and enduring Greg's donation as a wife. Thankfully, my cell phone buzzed.

"COVID test negative," was the text. I could leave the cab of my car! I could join Beau.

"Step at a time," I thought. I chose to wear the Momma hat. For the next few days, this transplant had to be the celebration for Beau that transplant is intended. It had to be the step forward that my son, our son, required. No more sideways. No more back-steps. I stepped into Children's Hospital, saturating my brain with thoughts of good, with energy for Beau, and I sent up prayers – deep intentional words with God – for my husband.

— 32 —
Transplant Day

Our hours in Children's Hospital leading up to transplant were unlike any hospital visit we had endured throughout the year before. This was less of an endurance and more like waiting for vacation. Beau maintained a lightness. I felt an aura around him of sheer hope, faith, and peace. He smiled broadly at every healthcare worker who entered his room, even the final administrator of his last pre–surgery COVID test.

"I don't know how I got nominated for this job," the sheepish nurse admitted. "I am so sorry, Beau. I need to thread this saline way back through your nose."

"No problem." Beau grinned and tipped his head upward. After the nurse collected her sample from the back of Beau's throat, his eyes streamed tears like a river. We agreed that the COVID test wasn't painful, just awkwardly invasive.

"Mom, can you grab me a tissue?" he laughed. Beau dabbed the corners of his watery eyes but remained content.

There was nothing that could shake Beau's spirit on the eve of his rebirth.

At 7:00 the next morning, two surgery techs came to Beau's room and all of us left for surgery. In the daylight, sunshine beamed through the windows of Children's Hospital and danced through the hallways. As we passed from one elevator to the next, the cheery sun warmed our travels. Something bigger than us guided the path as it had guided our entire journey. The whole trip to the surgery floor probably took eight minutes. Beau sat upright in his rolling bed with heightened awareness. He didn't lean back against the bed, but instead took in every sight. This was the culmination of so much pain and such despair, and our nerves and skin and eyelids and goose pimples stood ready for the change of a transplant.

Once we reached pre-op, Beau and I discussed that neither of us had ever been so awake. He exuded calm. It didn't come across to me as a cover-up. I didn't think he was hiding an anxious stomach or nervous butterflies. The same steadiness that had guided Beau through kidney failure was guiding him toward kidney freedom.

Beau leaned forward and whispered, "I can't wait to eat mashed potatoes again."

"The little things are the big things," I thought.

I smiled, letting my eyes settle over the perfection of Beau. His brown tousled hair, the small scar on his right cheek, his long, slim fingers that matched the shape and size of my Daddy's hands, his feathery eyelashes, the mole beneath his bottom lip, and even his Adam's apple. With the passing moments, I took in every bit of Beau. The next time I saw him, he would be changed.

Beau's surgeon greeted us, apologizing for being completely masked. She said that she hadn't had a lot of surgeries since the start of the pandemic, but that before she had left home to perform Beau's transplant, she had told her two-year-old son that she was going back to work to give another boy a new life.

"My little guy has no idea that you are twenty and not two," she explained to Beau, "but he knows about medicine and giving people hope."

"Well then, let's do this," Beau replied.

"I'll see you soon." I smiled, but was utterly choking on the air in the room.

I felt like I might never breathe again, the deep breath of a day without worry. I don't remember walking from pre-op to the waiting room.

While Beau was in surgery, he was assigned a number. I could follow his number, from the parent's waiting room, on a screen that would update such things as the progression from pre-op to mid-surgery, to recovery. At first, I selected a blue vinyl chair where I stared directly at the update screen. Sitting, watching, it felt like counting grains of salt. It was impossible. During my initial twenty minutes waiting, Beau's pre-op status did not change. I decided to walk. Because of pandemic regulations, there was only me and one other set of parents in the waiting room. It was ghostly empty, and I felt very lonely. I nodded at the other parents; they too were simply going through the motion of waiting. Each of us diverted our eyes to avoid a pointless interaction.

Just one quick ride, down on a glass elevator from where I waited, was the hospital foyer. I could leave through the big, heavy glass doors for a wave of fresh air, and I did. Within just a few steps, I landed on a concrete walkway that literally wound its way between the two physical buildings where my two people – my tribe – lay undergoing separate surgeries.

I immediately lifted my eyes toward Greg's hospital. It wasn't University Hospital; it was Greg's hospital. For the moment, I only thought of him and his team. The sunshine felt so good!

I closed my eyes and lifted my chin.

"Okay, Greg," I whispered. "You got this."

I took two more quick laps around and between the hospitals and returned to check Beau's number in the queue. The board said he was still in pre-op.

As I leafed through community magazines, I found a copy of *Good Housekeeping* from 2017. Anytime I visited a doctor's office, it astounded me how long certain magazines could linger in a waiting room. They almost took on lives of their own. I started to wonder, in fact, if I had ever seen a *Good Housekeeping* magazine anywhere besides a waiting room or on my grandma's bedside table. I felt eager to let my mind drift. I thought about my grandma and how she loved to read recipes in either *Good Housekeeping* or *Woman's Day*. After that, I counted the tiles around the little table in the kids' section of the waiting room.

"Casey?" The kidney center's social worker sat down beside me. "I am so excited for Beau! And how are you holding up?"

"I am doing okay." I replied. "So good to see you!"

Sarah, the social worker, saw Beau about once each week when he was at the hospital for dialysis. She had been great about checking in on his schoolwork and reminding him that he was a human, not a machine. With her tendency for dressing casually and laughing with great freedom, Sarah had a very calming presence in the Kidney Center.

"We're gonna miss your Beau in dialysis," she shared.

There are six chairs and six hemodialysis machines in the kidney center. It isn't huge. It is one big, sunny room with a team of dialysis nurses who cared for Beau hour after hour, week after week, and month after month for 300 days. The nurses knew the small things about Beau and the big things about Beau: that Rice Krispy bars were a sweet treat he rarely turned down, that in ten months as a dialysis patient, Beau always showed-up, that he had the patience of a grandpa when it came to listening to two of the younger boys in dialysis tell and retell knock-knock jokes, and that Beau was the real deal.

I sensed the feel of community when I sat with Beau during his treatments.

"You know Beau almost always eats lunch while he's here." Sarah said. "And one of our other patients who uses a feeding tube rather than eating by mouth: It never fails: he'll order a burger from the cafeteria if Beau orders a burger. He can't eat the burger, but he wants to be like Beau. So, they both order burgers and they sit together."

I smiled. "Oh my gosh!. Thank you so much for stopping to visit."

When I glanced back up, Beau's surgeon was standing right in front of me.

"Beau okay?" I asked.

"Everything's going great." She answered.

I sensed my jaw release, and I sat back hard against the bench. I was stunned to see her.

"Your husband's kidney has been removed, "she explained, "and it's a lovely kidney.

His surgeon just sent over a picture."

As calmly as if she were showing me a snapshot of her toddler, Beau's surgeon busted out her iPhone and showed me Greg's kidney.

"I have no idea what to look for," I explained. "Thank you, though, for showing me." The photo looked like the inside of my mouth, like a lot of gum tissue, or like the underside of my tongue – not at all gory.

She laughed. "It is very pink, isn't it?"

The surgeon pointed out the working parts of Greg's kidney

and said it was on its way across the parking lot to Beau. For weeks, I had wanted to name the kidney. I teased Beau about all the things we could call it: Beast or Arendo (for a particularly awesome Rockies baseball player). Beau wouldn't have it. In my mind, as the kidney was driven from one hospital to the next, I called it "Super G."

"I wanted you to know things are going well." She finished and rested her hand briefly on my shoulder before heading back to be with Beau. I also learned the new kidney would be placed in the front of Beau's abdomen, and not in the biologically normal kidney position.

I thought the surgeon was an absolute rock star. Once she left the waiting room and walked back to surgery, I estimated that I had about an hour before there would be another update. Again, the outdoors was my retreat. I made my way back to the glass escalator and out the front doors of the foyer, to a spot in the grass where I could see both hospitals. It was quite warm for April, and my short sleeve shirt was perfect. It was an instant where everything felt perfect in a way I hadn't felt perfection since Beau's diagnosis. I sat in the grass and said, "God, thank you."

I felt the way I felt the day after my wedding to Greg – the first whole day that I was someone's wife. I felt like the big work and the big worry was done. I felt a perfection and completion like I'd felt when I saw Bailey's perfectly round newborn head the first time, I became a Momma. My feeling during those transplant day moments in the sun was the same feeling I'd had only a couple of times in my life. The major difference was that those other times when I had felt such a completeness in my soul, I had felt it for myself. On Transplant Day, I felt complete goodness for Beau.

One hour later, I returned to the waiting room and found a new seat in a third sitting area where I could sit and watch the screen that should be updating Beau's progress at any moment. By 1 p.m., there was no update. Beau's number still listed that he was in surgery. My sense of calm was fading. I felt it fade. I hadn't received an update for three hours following my chat with Beau's surgeon. Momma texted. Bailey texted. Each of them had been alerted that Greg was in Recovery. Hospital protocols required that I not be the main point of contact for both of my family members as they underwent parallel surgery. In my heart though, I felt like the main point of contact; I felt like the main connection. But on paper, I was Beau's person, and Momma and Bailey were Greg's people. Having Greg out of surgery was positive. But what was taking so long for Beau?

Who do you ask about your child, when there is no one to ask about your child? I walked in circles around the waiting area. Earlier that morning, a volunteer had briefly sat behind an information desk. Her presence had been a nice glimpse of normalcy. By late afternoon, the volunteer was gone, and so was the other family who had been waiting for their child as I waited for mine. The physical emptiness inside the hospital walls did not create calm. My emotions got so high and dipped so low. I scribbled on a notepad I found in my wallet that I had never felt as personally unimportant as I felt then. It had been light, and now it was dark. The perfection I had felt, sitting in the sun after chatting briefly with Beau's surgeon, had slowly faded over the afternoon. Perfection faded into the anonymity of being a mom who waited alone for seven hours. My head was all over the place. My heart was full, and my heart was broken. At 3:30 p.m., a nurse came to find me in the waiting room.

"Beau's mom?" She asked.

"Yes. Yes. It's me." I stood up.

"Beau's recovering nicely. He is very polite." She told me.

"Is he awake then?" I reasoned.

"Oh yeah. Come on back." The nurse motioned for me to follow her toward the Intensive Care Unit. I knew this would be our home for at least the first night following transplant. I walked quickly.

"He is the sweetest patient. He was awake before they wheeled him in here," she explained, "and he smiled and thanked me for a couple of ice chips."

Once I spotted Beau, lying flat, attached to multiple IVs, and being monitored by a single nurse who sat right at his bedside, I had a tangible sense of life's fragility. I stepped right up to his bedside and was calmed by the warmth of Beau's breath and his skin.

"How are you, Buddy?" I whispered. I wasn't sure where to touch him. I gently held his foot. No needles. No bandages. Just a foot.

He lifted his left hand and gave me a thumb's up.

"I love you a lot." I said.

"Love you, too." Beau answered. He always answered. He never clicked off the phone or drove out of the driveway, he never left mad or forgot to acknowledge my words, and Beau always had time to love. That he loved me? That was never, ever in question.

— 33 —
Signs of Hope

On our fourth night in the hospital following Beau's successful transplant, the sound of sirens had continually grown louder. By about 8 p.m., Beau and I could hear sirens of every type – the long call of fire engines and the loud alarm of ambulances – as the conglomeration of noise floated up to our room six floors off the ground. It had been a remarkable Friday.

Every one of Beau's multiple IVs was removed. He had been weaned off of morphine for pain and took Tylenol by mouth only if he really needed it. The doctors and I encouraged him to take the Tylenol *before* he needed it, and mostly, Beau obliged. During an excellent follow-up discussion with Beau's surgeon, I learned that Beau's transplant surgery had not been abnormally long at seven-plus hours. She explained that because she removed one of his useless kidneys, called a nephrectomy, the transplant took additional time. After the fact, Beau's extra time in surgery seemed like a no-brainer, but in the middle of my isolation the day of surgery, the seven hours of waiting was the heaviest weight I had carried alone, period.

"Mom, you should look out the window and see what's going on." Beau prodded.

The sirens continued to wail.

"I will in just a minute," I replied. I carried my phone to Beau's bedside to show him pictures from earlier in the day. "Look how fun this picture is! I still can't believe so many of your friends showed up at the hospital!"

The best part of our Friday had been just after lunch, when I received a text from Beau's friend, Sophia, who asked if Beau could come to the window and look at the signs she and others from Regis were holding. When I told Beau his friends were outside, he rolled to one side of his hospital bed and eased into a standing position. He said that not only could he come to the window, but to text Sophia that he and I were heading down to the foyer.

"We're heading downstairs?" I asked, stunned.

"Yep. I can do it." Beau answered.

I texted Sophia that we were on our way to the elevator.

She texted "What?! So psyched!"

When Beau and I reached the entrance to Children's, we were both wearing masks and Beau was slightly stooped over from the pain of his incision. Just outside the hospital, in front of the glass doors, ten of Beau's closest college friends stood with signs of encouragement. When I saw them, I cried. The nurses who manned the doors to the hospital, instituting COVID regulations, cried. The ten friends cheered. While I cried, I laughed because two of Beau's friends held up a handmade sign that read: "URINE our thoughts."

Beau touched his hand to his heart. COVID regulations mandated he could not hug his friends, but he stood six feet away from them and said their coming to the hospital "means everything." It was amazing!

That evening, Beau looked at the pictures on my cell phone

and said that he would decide if we shared them on Facebook. He studied the signs and the smiles on the faces of his buddies.

"How cool was that?" Beau remarked.

"So cool." I replied. "Let me look and see why so many sirens."

I walked to the window and looked below. For as far as I could see, which was nearly two blocks, a line of fire trucks, police cars, and ambulances lined the streets surrounding the hospital. Outside of the vehicles, EMTs and police officers stood next to their vehicles clapping loudly.

"It's because of COVID!" I realized. "They're out here honoring the doctors and the nurses."

"Ah, I bet the little kids in the hospital love this!" Beau replied. He slowly made his way across the room to the window. The sight below was inspiring! Pressing our noses against the glass, Beau and I together counted sixteen emergency vehicles.

> **"What a send-off, Beau!" I looked at my precious son and smiled.**

The following morning, we would be released from the hospital, released to a new way forward. Beau would likely often wonder and worry about the health of his new kidney, and about the results of lab work that would continue through his adult life, but my great hope was that this kidney – "Super G" – would continue to be an awesome match for an awesome adventure.

Afterward

Beau insisted he felt fine. "You sound sniffly?" I worried over speaker phone. "All good here." He said, again.

It was October. Six months post-transplant. Six good months. Six great months!

COVID was on everyone's mind. Beau wore both a cloth and paper mask anytime he was in a public place. Transplant recovery also enabled us to spend more days than usual at home. Beau put together 3-D puzzles and sat on the back deck with our dogs; he closed his eyes and partook of the hot summer sun that is unique to Colorado mornings. Greg wandered around in front of the house watering his roses and thinking about being back on the jobsite. Watching him get out of bed and wince at the pain of his incision made me love him more every morning.

The days were ultimately very peaceful. Friends sent us a glorious number of take-out, Steak, potatoes and pizza. Beau could suddenly eat a normal diet and bathed in the normalcy of that.

Quinny B's mother even dropped off two freezer size bags of banana chocolate chip muffins, because bananas (which had *not* been part of a kidney friendly diet) were back in Beau's belly!

A few weeks before Beau headed back to Regis University, we took a causal road trip to Grand Teton National Park where

Beck and I kept up with Dad and Brother on our mountain bikes simply because the older two were recovering from major surgery. It was a minor perk. However, who fell off their bike seat while the four of us rested along a simple trail? That was me. Not even moving. Somewhere in the Tetons is a tiny diamond I knocked out of my wedding ring on that ridiculous fall. Beau was thriving. I wouldn't trade it.

Here's the thing: no one just "gets" a kidney transplant. People who receive an organ donation accept a new shot at life and new rules. I understand, now, why the initial vetting is so strenuous. Each morning at 9:00am, and each evening at 9:00pm, Beau takes a concoction of anti-rejection medicines. He will take these, twice daily, for the rest of his long life. In the few minutes required, Beau stops everything and takes his medicines, because they are his second chance. Two of the immunosuppressive drugs Beau takes are Tacrolimus (Tacro) and Mycophenolate. Through weekly and later monthly blood draws, including a Renal Panel, Beau's transplant nurse and a nephrologist regulate his Tacro.

Once back on campus, even though Beau "felt fine" and was a religious mask wearer, he tested positive for Covid. Along with the positive Covid test, Beau's mid-October renal panel showed he was positive for a virus called BK. On the one hand, Beau catching Covid in an immunosuppressed body seemed inevitable. On the other hand, I felt like he had dodged the virus for so long he might be immune to it. Remember, I am the same Momma who thought Beau would outgrow Lupus. If there is such a thing as ignorant bliss, Beau's Covid diagnosis rattled my bliss to the concrete floor. The next ten days got weird.

Big sister Bailey showed up big time. Beau couldn't come home with Covid, because none of us were yet eligible for the vaccine and Greg was still vulnerable. Beau couldn't stay in his dorm room either. We were faced with a true ethical dilemma, because our 20-year-old transplant recipient also couldn't live out of his tiny Mazda van for a week. Texts flew between Bailey, Beau and me. Then, during her lunch break from a real-life post-college career type of job, Bailey reserved a hotel room in Denver. She stocked the room with snacks, like Smartfood white cheddar popcorn and Smart Water, and texted Beau to meet her in the hotel parking lot.

"Don't forget I'm a working girl." She texted, and that meant Beau better get there and put a move on it.

Once parked, Bailey placed the room keycard on her hood and climbed back behind the wheel. She shut her driver's side door tightly. It wasn't long before Beau's grey Mazda could be seen ambling into the lot. Always an ultra-cautious driver, I can hear Bailey inside her head repeating "get here already Grampa." Which Beau eventually did. As Bailey retold the story, the two siblings exchanged a wave. She blew Beau a kiss. He placed two medical grade masks over his nose and mouth, donned surgical gloves, left his van, scooped the keycard quickly off Bailey's hood and briskly headed to the room where he would isolate for the next week.

Meanwhile, Beau's Nephrologist was contemplating how to treat *his* BK. This is a virus most of us carry in our urinary track or even bladder. As I understand it, for folks who are not immunocompromised, BK requires no treatment. Beau's team of doctors even suspected Greg's transplanted kidney had carried the BK over. Regardless of the root cause, Beau's BK count was too high. In-check BK is 375 copies/mL or lower. With the onset of Covid, Beau's BK count was more than one million.

"We're seeing this in some transplant patients." Beau's nurse typed. "Covid may exacerbate BK."

I thought this was big news. This was *new* news. The pandemic was showing doctors unique correlations between viruses on a continuum. Sure enough, when I ran a Google search, I came up with only two documented cases of kidney transplant patients whose BK numbers skyrocketed after Covid. The two documented cases were in England – on a whole other continent! I devoured what little information I found. My biggest question was this:

Had COVID caused anyone to lose their graft (new kidney)? Because the data was so new, the answer was inconclusive.

"Inconclusive isn't good enough." I complained to Greg over dinner.

"Well, the data doesn't say they lost their kidney." He pointed out, between forkfuls of rice.

Touché.

The super-heightened caretaker in me had been given a six-month break – in a sense I had a free–pass from worry. Now, I considered it cancelled. BK and COVID brought the intensity right back. My brain had muscle memory. With Beau isolating in a measly hotel room, and my email lighting up with correspondence from his transplant nurse, I felt some action had to be taken. How could we squelch the BK. Troubleshooting always hit me as a group activity and I also felt partially responsible for finding solutions. Since I could not personally prescribe my child medicine, I searched for the next best thing: supplements.

Supplements are powerful. They should never be used without consulting your doctor. I found this point to be beautifully articulated when I once discussed, with Beau's Rheumatologist, giving my son Turmeric. I thought Turmeric was a kind of forward thinker's vitamin C.

"Nope." She said, glad I had asked.

She went on to explain that Turmeric can jolt the immune

system, or fire it up in a way. Beau already had a confused immune system, because his rheumatologist hypothesized, he had Lupus. With Lupus, Beau's immune system attacked his own body and I understood, suddenly, that an immune system already on the attack might look and act like a monstrosity with the help of Turmeric. From this conversation, I learned to be careful with supplements. And with caution as my guide, I found one vitamin was mentioned in two articles as a significant weapon against BK.

Who doesn't love cinnamon toast? Cinnamon bears? Cinnamon apple cider? Cinnamon is a derivative of Ceylon, or cinnamon bark, and some patients with viruses have luck beating the virus with a combination of Ceylon pills and medical intervention. Cinnamon is an anti-viral, which doesn't work through the immune system, and that seemed positive in Beau's case.

I sent a lengthy email to Beau's transplant nurse, asking if his nephrologist thought it was safe to give Beau Ceylon pills. The wait ensued. For two long afternoons I drummed my fingernails against the wood in front of my computer, and refreshed my email every twenty minutes, hoping for an answer.

The emailed reply regarding Ceylon came in the form of a Yes with an addendum – Beau's nephrologist would also be cutting back on his immunosuppressives and prescribing Leflunomide. Again, Bailey showed up big.

To the parent of a transplant patient, cutting back on any medication that seems to be working can sound, well, ridiculous. Beau's body wasn't rejecting his new kidney. I didn't like the idea of cutting back on Tacro. Beau's nephrologist thought that he needed less immunosuppressive medicine to beat the BK, because immunosuppressive drugs cause white blood cells not to work as well in their fight against infection. BK was an infection.

Bailey, still geographically closest to Beau at her *real job* in

North Denver, picked up the new prescription and a burrito bowl from Wahoo's Fish Tacos. During her lunch break, she took both items to Beau in quarantine and hung them in a bag from the hallway doorknob. My insides beamed with pride for her generous heart. She simply served others unflinching. From sleeping on church floors in Alaska where she served homeless families, to visiting an orphanage in Ghana where she held tight to an abandoned boy whose head, she remembered, was the size of two cantaloups atop his withering body. Bailey loved with her whole heart.

"How's it going, buddy?" I texted Beau.

"Still feel fine. I'm sleeping a lot." Beau's version of Covid was mild.

We basically repeated this same pattern of texting every three hours for six days.

If things felt monotonous to me, I couldn't imagine how it felt for him to be in the same tiny room so many hours – stuck. Quarantine was a symptom of living within a Pandemic. Covid was big, the entire world lived inside of Covid's shell. Not just my little family, and I felt like one tiny snowflake in the snow globe of a Pandemic blizzard. Late one night I texted Beau philosophically.

"How do you keep going every day, buddy?" I asked.

Blinking dots showed he was typing.

He answered my question on his end, but he didn't send it. Life works like that for Beau.

I'd have to philosophize on my own. Beau had his answers. He didn't much care who else understood them. He has never been about explaining. He has always been about doing. My thoughts retreated to Beau's first wasted day of Chemo; to stopping at Ace Hardware along our drive home with the ridiculous mission of buying an axe, because being outdoors, cleaning the forest, and existing in the wild were the ways Beau kept going *that* day.

Throughout his battle with kidney failure and then the unknown effects of Covid on a transplanted kidney, Beau became a master at finding contentment and resting in it.

My son, this survivor and I, we're different. I feel the need to throw every thought and idea out into the universe. Beau needs to find contentment within himself. Self-preservation – self-appreciation – it doesn't matter what label I use, Beau has it.

After the long pause, I typed, "Well, *you* are really good at being content wherever you are. Proud of you."

"This bed is aamazinggg." He typed. That would be it until tomorrow.

I continue to be the one who thinks it and speaks it. If I say it, or type it, or drag words along my notebook with a sharpie, I believe I am manifesting my own destiny.

Beau doesn't feel the need to shout the day's promise from the rooftops, though I feel I am failing the day if I don't' do just that. This battle with Covid, even after I thought the hardest work of *actually getting* a transplant was behind us, proved kidney recipients must be vigilant. Beau's BK virus was sticky.

Once he left quarantine, Beau and I returned to our practice of visiting Children's Hospital for biweekly infusions. The next treatment for persistent BK was intravenous immunoglobulin (IVIG). Sitting together in infusion rooms, and studying the Colorado sky through wide open windowpanes, was familiar. We remained masked-up for the four-hour infusions and the masks, too, became secondary.

I retreated to Greg's pre-transplant motto: these infusions were the next step. Step at a time. Spending any amount of energy wondering, "Why Beau?" or complaining "Not this again" was old news. It had been done before.

The BK panels couldn't be run with the rest of Beau's

bloodwork at Children's and were farmed out to an externa lab. We had to wait three or four days from his blood draws to see if the BK numbers were going down. The number we could see almost immediately was Creatinine. I hated to look. Following the transplant, Beau's Creatinine had rested at 1.8, which for him was going to be an excellent resting place. Creatinine could live at 1.8 in Beau's body for a long time. The highest point his Creatinine reached while his body fought off Covid and BK was 2.7. My heart rose and fell with the Creatinine numbers.

In the very back of my mind I held onto the words from an email Beau's transplant nurse sent during his quarantine. She wrote that he could have a kidney biopsy to show just how much damage the BK was inflicting (if any) on his new kidney.

"Nope." I had replied. *No way, no how, what the heck are you even thinking.* "We're just six months post-transplant. Let's not start down that road…"

And then, after all the attacks had been mounted, Leflunomide ingested, Tacro reduced, IVIG infused, and Ceylon tablets swallowed, Beau received a miracle report. Finally, FINALLY, the BK retreated. His final BK count for the latest round of blood work was down from the millions to just under 500 copies/mL When a BK count is 375 or below, it is considered insignificant.

I prayed, "Thank you, God. Beau is healthy, strong and able."

Greg, Beck, and I had been gathered around the kitchen table watching football. Life in the Gent house was back to the three of us. For a moment I closed my eyes and settled on the idea that while Beau had learned to rest in contentment, my purpose was to exist in gratitude.

"Thankful for you," I whispered to Beck.

And grateful for the journey. . .

About the Author

CASEY BRADLEY GENT is a Colorado native, wife, and mother to three beloved children.

In 1995, one year after graduating from Colorado State University with degrees in Journalism and Speech Communications, Casey opened Snowshoe Studios photography. As the owner of this boutique studio, Casey has photographed presidents Clinton and Obama, two Super Bowls, numerous NFL and USA volleyball superstars, skating icon Peggy Fleming, countless intimate weddings, and thousands of family portraits. She still operates her studio and freelances for the Denver Broncos and local newspapers. Casey is an outdoor enthusiast who loves to run, hike, and play with her dogs and reindeer in the Colorado mountains. When Casey's son, Beau, was diagnosed with Lupus at thirteen years old, she became his fierce protector and medical advocate. Over the course of Beau's illness, Casey experienced the heartache and loneliness that comes with seeing a child suffering. She often felt helpless. During Beau's medical journey, she longed for a community or even a guidebook on how to get through the completely crushed feelings that came with Beau's diagnosis. While sitting in numerous hospital chairs, Casey began to write a narrative of her experience. Casey's journey as momma to a critically ill child ultimately revealed the importance of finding hope and joy in the little things and understanding that feeling wrecked does not equate to being broken. Her experience at a parent caretaker and witness to Beau's uplifting journey are captured in her work, *The Match and The Spark*.

CPSIA information can be obtained
at www.ICGtesting.com
Printed in the USA
BVHW032316130223
658422BV00004B/81